THE
grace—filled
HOMESTEAD
COOKBOOK

LANA STENNER

TEN PEAKS PRESS
EUGENE, OR

Published in association with Illuminate Literary Agency, www.illuminateliterary.com.

Cover design by Faceout Studio, Amanda Hudson
Interior design by Faceout Studio, Paul Nielsen
Photography by Lana Stenner

For bulk or special sales please call 1-800-547-8979. Email: Customerservice@hhpbooks.com

▲. TEN PEAKS PRESS is a federally registered trademark of The Hawkins Children's
LLC. Harvest House Publishers, Inc., is the exclusive licensee of this trademark.

The Grace-Filled Homestead Cookbook
Copyright © 2023 by Lana Stenner
Published by Ten Peaks Press, an imprint of Harvest House Publishers
Eugene, Oregon 97408

ISBN 978-0-7369-8478-2 (pbk.)
ISBN 978-0-7369-8479-9 (eBook)

Library of Congress Control Number: 2023930955

Printed in China

24 25 26 27 28 29 30 31 / RDS–FO / 10 9 8 7 6 5 4 3 2

This cookbook is dedicated
to my precious family

Dad, Mom, and CJ
Colton, Cameron, Isaiah, Sophia,
Madalyn, Jadyn, and Riley Rose

"You Are My Sunshine"

Contents

Ingredients for the Good Life

Many of us have followed the desire to get back to the basics in life, including the joy of preparing meals for friends and family with fresh and seasonal ingredients. I come from a long line of homesteaders and backyard farmers. My great-grandparents crossed the plains in a covered wagon to stake their ground in Missouri and begin living off the land. Once cities crowded in, my branch of the family tree could be found in a typical suburban neighborhood. However, my mama's backyard strawberry patch and container herb garden kept the family tradition of digging in the dirt and eating what we grew.

Over the years, our family has shifted back to the basics of intentional, simple living and eating quality food. We moved to the Grace-Filled Homestead more than twenty years ago and have come to believe that cooking is not a chore but a gift for a family, especially if the fresh ingredients have come out of the backyard.

Connection, bonding, and slowing down all happen in the kitchen with your loved ones. Whether you have a flock of chickens to produce eggs daily, a fruit orchard and a thriving vegetable garden, or a downtown loft apartment with planter boxes, quality local ingredients are the key to the flavor and experience of a homestead. If you're not growing your own food, a trip to the Saturday morning farmer's market is pure joy and a way to savor healthy, beautiful offerings.

As we journey through the calendar, the goodness of the seasons will shine through. On this adventure we will taste foraged mushrooms and edible spring wildflowers. Summer brings traditional Kansas City barbecue and heirloom tomatoes. As the temperatures cool and the fall leaves turn brilliant colors, the mulled apple cider and pumpkin-spiced

Experiencing the good life is as simple as preparing delicious food with the ones you love.

flavors come alive. And finally, as the winter months approach, there is nothing better than a steaming bowl of soup, a decadent dessert, and a cozy fire.

Cooking is a beautiful ingredient for the good life, even more than travel and lavish possessions, because it cultivates deep relationships, allows for an appreciation of natural flavors, and gives you an avenue to creativity and fulfillment. Good food and conversation can bring healing from the pressures of the world. Chopping vegetables with a loved one is medicine for your body and soul.

Finally, let's build an apothecary pantry of your very own. In the last chapter we'll learn from our grandparents' methods of preserving food and keeping our bodies healthy. Making your own sourdough bread is especially rewarding when you slather on a homemade jam. Fruit syrups and fizzy kombucha will put a smile on your face. And curating your own spice cabinet, seasonings, and fresh ingredients opens the door to experiencing life's simple pleasures in countless ways.

I'm so thankful you'll be joining me on this journey around the sun as we embark on the good life, which overflows with family and friends, fresh ingredients, and foodie flavors that nourish your soul in every season.

Spring

Spring at the Grace-Filled Homestead is a time of births and new beginnings. After a long, brutal winter, we are ready to shed the heavy sweaters, Carhartt jackets, and wool hats for a warm breeze while we watch the robins in their nests. It's exciting to see seeds sprouting, baby goats leaping off logs, sunshine pouring in on the porch swing, and the chicks hatching.

It's a time of hard work. We prepare the gardens, spring-clean the coop, and make room for upcoming hay deliveries. We repair fences, turn the compost, and tend the bee apiary. We welcome the outdoor work, an afternoon foraging for mushrooms and gathering wildflower blooms. There is nothing as delightful as seeing the first daffodils and tulips pop through the soil.

Spring is filled with holidays, baby and wedding showers, Mother's Day brunches, and the blessed start to the cookout season. These gatherings are centered around family, friends, and food made from scratch. As the celebrations start making their way outside, they always end with a walk out to the gardens and a baby goat snuggle.

As we finish off the last of our canned veggies and winter jam, it's the beginning of our fresh farm-to-table food season. Our recipes are filled with fresh herbs, foraged mushrooms, and edible flowers. I absolutely love spring.

Welcome, spring, you are pure joy!

LILAC-GLAZED DONUTS

With subtle hints of vanilla and lilac, this donut recipe is the perfect addition to your spring brunch. And you avoid the hassle of rising yeast. This cake donut is rustic, shallow fried, and topped with a floral glaze—yes please! This earthy donut is less sweet than other baked goods, so feel free to eat two.

PREP TIME: 25 minutes › TOTAL TIME: 55 minutes › YIELD: 12 Servings

DIRECTIONS

To prepare for the process, fill a 3-inch-deep saucepan with 1 inch of vegetable oil. Line a baking tray with a wire rack and paper towels for the donuts to drain, and set aside.

In a medium bowl, combine the flour, sugar, baking powder, baking soda, salt, cinnamon, and lilac blooms and set aside.

In a large bowl, combine the buttermilk, melted butter, vanilla, and eggs. Gradually whisk the dry ingredients into the wet until a sticky dough is formed. Transfer the dough to a lightly floured work surface. Use your palms to press the dough into roughly a 12-inch rectangle about ½ inch thick.

Heat the oil over low-to-medium heat for 5 minutes. While the oil is heating, cut out 12 donuts and holes using 3-inch and 1-inch round cookie cutters. Test the oil temperature with a donut hole. If the oil is hot enough, the dough will puff up and be golden brown after cooking 1 minute per side. When the oil is ready, carefully drop the donuts into the oil in batches, taking care not to crowd the pan. Allow the donuts to fry for about 1 to 2 minutes per side or until golden brown.

Once the donuts are done, carefully remove them from the oil using a spider basket utensil. After transferring the cooked donuts to your wire rack, repeat the process with the remaining donuts until they are all cooked.

While the donuts are cooling, whisk together the powdered sugar and milk for the glaze. Once the donuts are completely cool, dip them into the glaze and return them to the wire rack. If you like an extra-thick glaze like we do, dip them again once the glaze has set a bit, and return them to the rack. Sprinkle with lilac flowers and serve.

INGREDIENTS

3½ cups flour

¾ cup sugar

½ cup lilac blossoms, stems removed

2 tsp. baking powder

½ tsp. baking soda

1 tsp. salt

1 tsp. cinnamon

¾ cup buttermilk

¼ cup butter, melted

1 tsp. vanilla extract

2 eggs

Vegetable oil for frying

GLAZE INGREDIENTS

1½ cups powdered sugar

2 T. milk

¼ cup lilac blossoms for garnish

ROASTED CORNED BEEF AND CABBAGE

Roasted corned beef is a family favorite for Saint Patrick's Day. If you're not a fan of this traditional Irish dish, it may be because you've only had it boiled. Roasting it brings out all the delicious flavors and allows you to cook the cabbage and potatoes all in one pan.

PREP TIME: 20 minutes > TOTAL TIME: 4 hours, 25 minutes > YIELD: 8 Servings

DIRECTIONS

Preheat the oven to 325°F and combine the spice mixture ingredients in a small, dry skillet. Place the skillet over medium heat for 2 minutes to slightly toast the spices. Remove them from the skillet, let them cool, and smash the spices on a cutting board with the bottom of a glass to release the flavors.

Place the corned beef in large roasting pan and add ½ inch of water. Add half the spice mixture to the top of the corned beef and the other half to the water. Cover the pan and place it in the oven to roast for 3 hours. Add whole potatoes to the roasting pan and cook for an additional 45 minutes. Add the cabbage to the pan and cook for 15 more minutes. Remove the pan from the oven and let the meat rest for 15 minutes. Slice the meat across the grain and then add it back to the roasting pan with the potatoes and cabbage. Serve straight from the roasting pan with mustard or horseradish, if desired.

INGREDIENTS

3 pounds corned beef brisket

8 red potatoes

1 large head cabbage, cut into small wedges

SPICE MIXTURE INGREDIENTS

1½ tsp. coriander seeds (cilantro seeds)

1 tsp. mustard seeds

1½ tsp. peppercorns

1 tsp. crushed red pepper flakes

¼ tsp. allspice

1 bay leaf, crushed

SUNSHINE ON MY SHOULDERS BENEDICT

Eggs Benedict is my all-time favorite breakfast dish, and it's all about the hollandaise sauce for me. At the Grace-Filled Homestead, we take it up a notch with the addition of lemon zest and a double dose of bacon. The buttery citrus flavors against the delicious bacon and toasted muffin are sure to make your heart sing.

PREP TIME: 15 minutes > TOTAL TIME: 30 minutes > YIELD: 6 Servings

DIRECTIONS

Preheat the oven to 400ºF. Coat a muffin pan with cooking spray. To simply poach the eggs, add 2 tablespoons of water to six cups of the muffin pan. Carefully crack an egg into each cup, keeping the yolk intact. Bake for 10 minutes. While the eggs are cooking, toast the English muffin halves and then slather them with butter.

To prepare your hollandaise sauce, add the egg yolks and lemon juice into your blender. Blend at medium speed for 45 seconds. The yolk color will lighten. With the blender running on medium, slowly pour very hot melted butter into the yolk mixture. Adding hot butter very slowly will cook the eggs without curdling them. Add cayenne pepper and 1 teaspoon of lemon zest and blend an additional minute before assembling the dish. We love our sauce thick, but if you like it thinner, add a tablespoon of hot water.

To assemble, place one toasted English muffin half on each plate and top with three slices of bacon. Carefully remove an egg from the muffin tin, gently pat the water off with a tea towel, and place the egg on the bacon slices. Generously add the hollandaise sauce, and top with chives and additional lemon zest. Serve warm.

INGREDIENTS

3 English muffins, cut in half

1 T. butter, for spreading

18 slices bacon, cooked

6 eggs

1 tsp. chopped fresh chives

HOLLANDAISE SAUCE INGREDIENTS

6 egg yolks

3 T. fresh lemon juice

1 cup butter, melted

Sprinkle of cayenne pepper

2 tsp. lemon zest, separated

BACON-WRAPPED ASPARAGUS

Delight your family and friends with a vegetable treasure covered in crispy bacon goodness. Bacon-wrapped asparagus is a treat for any holiday meal or special occasion. This simple five-ingredient recipe can be ready in less than a half hour. We bake ours in the oven, but we also love the air fryer method for extra-crispy bacon.

PREP TIME: 15 minutes > TOTAL TIME: 30 to 45 minutes > YIELD: 8 Servings

INGREDIENTS

2 lbs. asparagus

1 tsp. salt

1 tsp. pepper

1 tsp. oil

1 lb. bacon

DIRECTIONS

Preheat the oven or grill to 400°F. Cut 1 inch off the end of each stalk, leaving the top point intact. Coat the stalks with oil, salt, and pepper. Collect five pieces of asparagus together and wrap them with a strip of bacon. If you like crispy bacon, take care to minimize areas where the bacon overlaps. A single layer will crisp quicker.

Place bacon-wrapped asparagus on a pan and bake for 15 minutes, then turn the bundles over and bake an additional 15 minutes or until the bacon is crispy. If tips are browning too much, cover them with foil while the bacon crisps. For crispier bacon, place the pan under the broiler for 2 minutes before serving. If you prefer the air fryer method, place prepared bacon-wrapped asparagus in the air fryer at 375°F for 10 to 15 minutes.

Optional: Serve with a side of hollandaise sauce (page 17).

SEVEN-LAYER SALAD

The seven-layer salad is a staple at our family gatherings, and it's one of the first dishes to run out. It has all the healthy layers of lettuce and vegetables with added layers of cheese and a creamy dressing. You can customize your layers, like we have in the past. However, these classic ingredients are the favorites at the Grace-Filled Homestead.

PREP TIME: 15 minutes > TOTAL TIME: 1 hour, 15 minutes > YIELD: 10 Servings

DIRECTIONS

Spread the lettuce evenly in the bottom of a glass bowl. Any bowl will work but seeing the layers through a glass dish makes serving more fun. Next, layer the red onions on top of the lettuce followed by the celery and then the peas. Combine the mayo and sour cream in a separate bowl, then carefully spread the mixture on top of the peas. Crumble the cooked bacon strips and add them to the dish. Add the final layer of shredded cheese. Cover the dish and chill in the refrigerator for 1 hour before serving.

INGREDIENTS

1 head of lettuce, shredded (we like iceberg or romaine)

1 large red onion, diced

4 celery stalks, sliced

1½ cups frozen peas, thawed

½ cup mayonnaise

½ cup sour cream

1 lb. cooked bacon

1 cup cheddar cheese, shredded

GARDEN-ART FOCACCIA

Focaccia is a delicious bread that can be served as an appetizer or alongside your favorite main dish. It's fun to get creative with the veggie and herb toppings to make your own artful masterpiece. Invite the kids to help in the creation process.

PREP TIME: 15 minutes > **TOTAL TIME: 1 hour, 50 minutes** > **YIELD: 6 Servings**

DIRECTIONS

Bloom the yeast and sugar in lukewarm water: Whisk it together and let it sit for 5 minutes or until it bubbles and foams. If it doesn't, your yeast may be expired. Check the date and start over. In a large bowl, combine the bubbly yeast mixture, flour, salt, and 1 tablespoon of the olive oil. The dough will be sticky. Form it into a ball, cover the bowl with plastic wrap, and let the dough rise in a warm spot for at least 30 minutes.

Coat a 9-inch round cake pan with 1 tablespoon of olive oil. Add the dough to the pan and stretch it to cover the bottom evenly. Cover the pan with plastic wrap and place it in a warm spot to allow the dough to rise for an additional 45 minutes.

Preheat the oven to 400°F. Dimple the dough with damp fingers, then drizzle the remaining tablespoon of olive oil, allowing it to fill the indentions in the dough. In a small bowl, whisk 1 egg yolk and lightly brush the egg wash on top of the dough.

Now for the fun part: Let your creative juices flow as you artfully arrange the herbs and vegetables on top of the dough to form a scene of flowers or other parts of a garden. Slightly push your art into the dough to secure it. Sprinkle salt over the top and bake for 15 minutes or until golden brown. Remove the focaccia from the pan, cool it on a baking rack, and enjoy!

INGREDIENTS

2¼ tsp. active dry yeast

½ tsp. sugar

½ cup lukewarm water

1¼ cups flour

½ tsp. salt

3 T. olive oil, separated

1 egg for wash

1 tsp. coarse salt

Favorite herbs, nuts, and veggies for focaccia topping: chives, parsley, thyme, and oregano for the greenery; peppers, cherry tomatoes, and olives for the blooms; olives and almond slivers for the bees; and a sprinkle of poppy seeds.

WILD-VIOLET HOT CROSS BUNS

Hot cross buns are a classic Easter tradition for many families. The sweet dough is covered in a vanilla icing cross. Our version includes foraged wild violets. These edible flowers poke through the grass even before our tulips do. We used to consider them weeds but now enjoy them in our recipes. My children grew up delighting in hot cross buns every spring, singing the song that goes with it.

PREP TIME: 25 minutes › TOTAL TIME: 3 hours, 20 minutes › YIELD: 24 Servings

INGREDIENTS

1¼ cups whole milk, divided

¾ cup sugar

4½ tsp. active dry yeast

¾ cup butter, melted

¼ tsp. salt

¼ tsp. cinnamon

4 eggs, lightly beaten

5½ cups flour, plus more for surface

¾ cup foraged violets, greens and stems removed

FROSTING INGREDIENTS

1 egg white

2 cups powdered sugar

½ tsp. vanilla extract

DIRECTIONS

Heat 1 cup of milk in a small saucepan over medium heat until it hits 110°F degrees on a thermometer. Fit a stand mixer with a dough hook and pour the milk into a mixer bowl. With the mixer on low, add the sugar, yeast, butter, salt, cinnamon, and eggs. Add the flour, 1 cup at a time, and knead until the mixture comes together in a soft, sticky dough. Continue kneading, scraping the mixer hook as needed, until the dough is smooth, about 5 minutes.

Add the violets and knead to incorporate. Turn the dough out onto a lightly floured surface and knead for an additional minute. Coat a large bowl with butter. Shape the dough into a ball and place it in the prepared bowl. Cover the bowl with plastic wrap and let the dough rise until doubled in size, about 1 hour.

Generously butter a baking sheet or dish. Turn out the dough onto a floured surface, knead it briefly, then divide it evenly into 4 pieces. Working with 1 piece at a time, divide each into 6 smaller pieces. Shape each of the 24 pieces into a tight ball and place them on the prepared sheet, spacing ½ inch apart. Cover the buns with plastic and let them rise in a warm spot until they have doubled in size and are touching, about 1 hour.

Preheat the oven to 375°F.

Whisk the egg white in a small bowl, then brush the tops of the buns with the egg-white wash. Bake, rotating the sheet halfway through, until the buns are golden brown, 20 to 22 minutes. Let them cool for 30 minutes. Whisk the remaining milk with the powdered sugar and vanilla. Spoon the icing into a pastry bag fitted with a ¼-inch round tip and pipe the icing on the buns in the shape of a cross. Garnish with additional violet blooms and serve.

THREE-CHEESE HASHBROWN CASSEROLE

This potato casserole is a crowd pleaser at any barbecue, potluck, or breakfast brunch. The creamy cheese melts into the delicious hashbrowns. The mild mushroom flavors add depth to this dish. This casserole is usually gone within minutes!

PREP TIME: 15 minutes › TOTAL TIME: 1 hour › YIELD: 12 Servings

DIRECTIONS

Preheat the oven to 350°F. Combine the hashbrowns, soup, cream cheese, Colby cheese, onion, sour cream, butter, salt, and pepper in a large bowl. Place in a greased 9 x 13-inch casserole dish. Top the potato mixture with the cheddar cheese. Bake for 45 minutes. Garnish with fresh chives and enjoy!

INGREDIENTS

30 oz. frozen shredded hashbrowns

1 (10.5 oz) can condensed cream of mushroom soup

4 oz. cream cheese, softened

1 cup Colby cheese, shredded

1 onion, chopped

1 cup sour cream

½ cup butter, melted

2 tsp. salt

1 tsp. pepper

¾ cup cheddar cheese, shredded

Chives for garnish

REDBUD SKYSCRAPER SHAKE

Making skyscraper shakes is a family affair at the Grace-Filled Homestead. Redbud blossoms are among our favorite edible flowers. Great-Grandma Rose loved to serve Neapolitan ice cream with the layers of strawberry, vanilla, and chocolate, so we are carrying on the tradition in shake form. The addition of redbuds and malted milk gives the shake a deeper flavor, which the entire gang can enjoy when it's served in a large flower vase. Don't forget the straws!

PREP TIME: 15 minutes > **YIELD: 6 Servings**

DIRECTIONS

Harvest and wash the redbud blossoms and remove all greenery. Add the 8 cups of Neapolitan ice cream, redbuds, milk, and malted milk powder to blender. Blend until smooth and pour into a large clean glass flower vase or pitcher. Top with whipped cream, fresh redbud blossoms, and straws for your favorite people.

INGREDIENTS

1/4 cup redbud blossoms plus more for garnish

2 quarts Neapolitan ice cream

½ cup milk

1 T. malted milk powder

1 cup whipped cream

LAVENDER LEMONADE WITH LAVENDER ICE CUBES

As the spring temperatures warm and the aromatic lavender plants bloom, we are drawn to the front porch, where we find a glass of sweet lemonade waiting. This recipe blends sweet lavender simple syrup with the tart lemon flavors for a beautiful drink that can be served at your fanciest brunch or as a treat after a muddy day of planting your gardens.

PREP TIME: 15 minutes > TOTAL TIME: 7 hours, 15 minutes > YIELD: 8 Servings

DIRECTIONS

First, make the ice cubes by rinsing your fresh lavender buds, removing the stems, and placing one bud at the base of each cube area in the tray. Fill each cube halfway with water and freeze for 3 hours. Then fill each cube compartment the rest of the way to the top with cold water. Freeze an additional 4 hours.

Make the lavender simple syrup while your ice is forming: Combine the water and sugar in a saucepan over medium heat, whisking until the sugar is dissolved. Remove from heat and stir in the honey and lavender. Let the mixture steep for 20 minutes. Strain the lavender out and chill the mixture for 1 hour.

Next, make the lemonade by combining the freshly squeezed lemon juice, water, and chilled lavender simple syrup. Chill for 1 hour. Serve over your prepared lavender ice cubes.

ICE CUBE INGREDIENTS

2 cups water

24 fresh lavender blooms

2 (12 cube) ice trays

SIMPLE SYRUP INGREDIENTS

1 cup water

1 cup sugar

1 T. honey

3 T. fresh or dried lavender

LEMONADE INGREDIENTS

2 cups freshly squeezed lemon juice

4 cups water

1 lemon, sliced

Prepared lavender simple syrup

CHICKEN SPIEDINI WITH LEMON SAUCE

Chicken spiedini, a foodie favorite, makes a wonderful main course for parties and family gatherings. The skewered garlic, cheese, and red pepper chicken are complemented by the delicious lemon sauce.

PREP TIME: 25 minutes > **TOTAL TIME: 3 hours, 45 minutes** > **YIELD: 8 Servings**

MARINADE INGREDIENTS

3 lbs. boneless, skinless chicken breasts

3 eggs

1 T. crushed garlic

1 tsp. salt

1 tsp. pepper

1 tsp. crushed red pepper flakes

SAUCE INGREDIENTS

3 cups lemon juice

1 cup olive oil

1 tsp. crushed garlic

¼ cup fresh basil, chopped

½ tsp. salt

¼ tsp. pepper

½ tsp. crushed red pepper flakes

BREADING INGREDIENTS

1 cup Italian breadcrumbs

1 cup grated Parmesan cheese

Zest of one lemon

DIRECTIONS

Cut the chicken into 2-inch cubes and place them in a large bowl. Mix the marinade ingredients together—eggs, garlic, salt, pepper, and red pepper flakes. Pour the marinade over the chicken, cover, and let it sit in the refrigerator for 3 to 4 hours. Meanwhile, combine all ingredients for the lemon sauce and refrigerate for 3 to 4 hours. Stir once an hour.

Preheat the grill to 300°F. Thread the chicken onto skewers.

Mix together the breadcrumbs, Parmesan, and lemon zest in a baking dish. Roll the chicken skewers in the breadcrumb mixture, coating them completely. Grill for 10 minutes, then brush both sides with the lemon sauce, and flip the skewer. Cook an additional 10 minutes or until the internal temperature reaches 165°F.

Remove the skewers from the grill and brush both sides of the chicken with lemon sauce. Serve the spiedini intact, with additional lemon sauce.

WILD MUSHROOM FRENCH ONION SOUP

Every spring our family forages the forest for wild mushrooms. Our favorite are the hard-to-find morels. This creamy cottagecore soup is reminiscent of the classic French onion, yet it has a few extra scrumptious ingredients. The wild mushrooms and goat cheese pair wonderfully with the French bread and Gruyère topping. If you can't find morels, any of your favorite wild mushrooms will work. If you are foraging, be sure to do your homework and know which ones are edible.

PREP TIME: 15 minutes > TOTAL TIME: 1 hour > YIELD: 6 Servings

DIRECTIONS

In a large soup pot, melt the butter over medium heat, add the thinly sliced onions, and sauté for 10 minutes. Add in the mushrooms and sauté for an additional 20 minutes. Add the beef broth, thyme, garlic, bay leaf, black pepper, Worcestershire, and honey. Bring to a boil, reduce heat, and simmer for 30 minutes.

Remove and discard the bay leaf and thyme. Stir in the goat cheese and simmer an additional 15 minutes. Meanwhile, slice the bread and brush it with olive oil. Broil 2 minutes per side or until golden. Ladle the soup into ceramic, oven-safe bowls. Add 2 slices of bread to each bowl. Sprinkle the Gruyère evenly over the bread in the bowls and broil until golden and bubbly.

INGREDIENTS

1 cup butter

3 large onions, peeled and thinly sliced

2 cups wild mushrooms, washed and sliced

8 cups beef broth

3 sprigs fresh thyme

1 T. minced garlic

1 bay leaf

¼ tsp. pepper

1 T. Worcestershire sauce

1 tsp. honey

4 oz. goat cheese

1 French baguette

1 to 2 T. olive oil

3 cups Gruyère cheese, shredded

WILDFLOWER VANILLA CRÈME CAKE

This is our signature cake at the Grace-Filled Homestead. It's not only fresh and beautiful but also delicious. The American buttercream icing is our favorite, and the edible flower petals are earthy, adding another level of depth to every bite. The edible flowers we use on this cake are lavender, calendula, pansies, violas, zinnias, chamomile, and echinacea.

PREP TIME: 30 minutes > TOTAL TIME: 1 hour, 5 minutes > YIELD: 10 Servings

DIRECTIONS

Preheat the oven to 350°F. Grease and flour three 6-inch round pans. In a bowl, cream together the cream cheese, sugar, and softened butter. Beat in the eggs, then add the vanilla. Combine the flour and baking powder, add it to the creamed mixture, and mix well. Finally, stir in the milk until the batter is smooth.

Pour 3 equal amounts of batter into the prepared pans. Bake for 20 minutes. Let the cakes cool on a wire rack for 15 minutes before removing them from their pans. Refrigerate the individual cakes for 3 hours before assembling. Create the icing by creaming together the butter, shortening, vanilla, milk, and powdered sugar. Once all the ingredients are blended on low, beat for 2 minutes on high speed to add fluffiness. Adjust the consistency by adding more milk or powdered sugar as needed.

To assemble the cooled cake, place one layer on a serving dish. Spread ¾ cup of icing across only the top of the cake, making a lip to hold in the lemon curd. Add half the lemon curd into the icing indention. Top with the next layer of cake and repeat the process with the icing and lemon curd. Once the final cake layer is on top, frost the top of the cake and give the sides a thin crumb coat using an offset spatula. Refrigerate the cake for 1 hour and then spread the remaining icing over the entire cake until smooth. Remove the backs and stems from the wildflowers, then add them to the cake to make your custom masterpiece.

INGREDIENTS

4 oz. cream cheese, softened

1 cup white sugar

½ cup butter, softened to room temperature

2 eggs

2 tsp. vanilla extract

1½ cups all-purpose flour

1¾ tsp. baking powder

½ cup milk

24 fresh edible flowers

¾ cup lemon curd

ICING INGREDIENTS

1½ cups salted butter

½ cup shortening

2 tsp. vanilla extract

⅓ to ½ cup milk, to desired consistency

4 cups powdered sugar

PEACH CHIPOTLE PULLED PORK

This sweet and spicy pulled pork steals the show at every barbecue or event it is served. You may already have the secret ingredients of peaches, soda, and liquid smoke in your kitchen. You don't need a smoker for the bursting barbecue flavor. This dish slow cooks in your oven while you go about your day.

PREP TIME: 15 minutes > TOTAL TIME: 6 hours, 15 minutes > YIELD: 8 Servings

DIRECTIONS

Preheat the oven to 300°F. Start the dish by distributing the peaches and syrup in the bottom of an oven-safe pot that has a lid. Then add the onion quarters and liquid smoke to the pot. Place the pork butt (which is a shoulder) on top of the onions. The fat side should be facing up.

Ready for the magic? Pour 1 can of Sprite over the top of everything. Then pour on the chipotle peppers with adobo sauce. The next step is purposely done after the liquid is poured so it doesn't wash off: Sprinkle the pork with the brown sugar, salt, and pepper. Cover the pot, put it in the oven, and cook for about 6 hours. You will want to turn the meat over with heavy duty tongs after 2 hours of cooking, let it cook 2 more hours, and then turn it back over for the final 2 hours. When it's done, the pork will be covered in a dark and delicious caramelization and be falling apart in juicy goodness.

Remove the meat, peaches, peppers, and onions from the pot and completely mix and shred everything together with a fork. Discard the bone and return the meat to the pot with a small amount of the juices. This will keep it moist. Add additional salt to taste.

The pulled pork can be served many ways, such as in enchiladas, tacos, or your morning egg scramble. However, our favorite is on a simple burger bun. It's the best barbecue sandwich around and makes cooking for big events a breeze!

INGREDIENTS

1 (6 to 10 lb.) pork butt (pork shoulder)

1 (15 oz.) can peeled and sliced peaches in syrup

2 yellow onions, quartered

1 tsp. liquid smoke

12 oz. Sprite

1 (14 oz.) can chipotle peppers in adobo sauce

½ cup packed brown sugar

2 tsp. coarsely ground sea salt

1 tsp. pepper

BLT DEVILED EGGS

Eggs are a go-to food on most homesteads, and ours is no exception. Deviled eggs are a classic addition to any family gathering. If you want to make a recipe amazing, just add bacon. This BLT version of deviled eggs will be wiped out in minutes.

PREP TIME: 20 minutes > TOTAL TIME: 20 minutes > YIELD: 12 Servings

DIRECTIONS

Slice hard-boiled eggs in half lengthwise. Place the egg yolks in a small bowl and the egg whites on a plate. Smash the yolks with a fork, then stir in the mayonnaise, mustard, vinegar, salt, and pepper until it is completely combined and smooth.

Use a spoon to add the yolk mixture back into each egg white. Cut the cherry tomatoes in half and roughly chop the bacon into ½ inch pieces. Top each deviled egg half with a cherry tomato half, bacon crumbles, and parsley leaves. Chill and serve cold.

INGREDIENTS

6 large hard-boiled eggs, cooled and peeled

3 T. mayonnaise

1 tsp. Dijon mustard

2 tsp. apple cider vinegar

Salt and pepper to taste

6 cherry tomatoes

3 strips cooked bacon

Fresh parsley to garnish

FRESH FRUIT BREAKFAST PIZZA

Our family first experienced fruit pizza while enjoying a bed and breakfast cabin in the mountains of Wyoming. The kiddos were tiny and gobbled up every morsel as if they hadn't eaten in days. Once we arrived home, we created our own version by replacing the biscuit crust with our favorite sugar cookie dough, and the rest was history. Seasonal fruit variations keep this breakfast fresh and delicious.

PREP TIME: 15 minutes › TOTAL TIME: 45 minutes › YIELD: 8 Servings

INGREDIENTS

16 oz. chilled sugar cookie dough

1 (8 oz.) pkg. cream cheese, softened

½ cup powdered sugar

8 oz. whipped cream

4 cups fresh fruit, sliced

DIRECTIONS

Preheat the oven to 350°F. Spread the cookie dough onto an ungreased 14-inch pizza pan. Bake for 15 minutes or until it is deep golden brown; set the pan on a wire rack to cool. In a bowl, beat the cream cheese and powdered sugar until smooth. Fold in the whipped cream, then spread the mixture over the cooled crust. Pat the fruit slices dry with a paper towel and arrange them on top in whatever fun pattern you desire. Chill until you are ready to serve and enjoy!

BROWNED-BUTTER SCALLOPS WITH ROSEMARY RISOTTO

Risotto is a dish we savor here. Anytime we can add herbs and scrumptious seafood to it, we do. Sautéing the scallops in browned butter adds an extra dimension of flavor to this meal. The creamy risotto with hints of rosemary complements the scallops wonderfully.

PREP TIME: 15 minutes > TOTAL TIME: 50 minutes > YIELD: 6 Servings

DIRECTIONS

In a medium saucepan, bring the broth to a simmer. Lower the heat and keep the broth on low. In a large saucepan over medium heat, add 3 tablespoons butter and the olive oil. Sauté the onion and cook until softened, about 5 minutes. Add in the garlic and cook for 5 minutes, stirring occasionally.

Add in the rice and stir until well-coated, about 2 minutes. You will notice the rice becoming translucent. Slowly ladle in the warm broth in increments, stirring regularly between additions and allowing the broth to be fully absorbed before adding the next ladleful. Repeat until the rice is creamy and all the broth is absorbed, about 20 minutes. Remove the pan from the heat and stir in the rosemary, Parmesan, salt, and pepper. Cover the rice with a lid or foil and let it rest for 5 minutes while you prepare the scallops.

Pat the scallops dry with a paper towel and season with salt and pepper. Heat a large pan with 4 tablespoons of butter on high heat. Let the butter brown before adding the scallops. Cook for 3 minutes undisturbed. When the scallops are mostly opaque, flip them, drain the scallop liquid, add the remaining 1 tablespoon of butter, and cook for 1 minute undisturbed until the scallops are completely opaque. Remove the scallops from the pan and serve on top of the bed of risotto.

INGREDIENTS

6 cups chicken broth

½ cup butter, divided

1 T. olive oil

1 cup onion, finely chopped

1 tsp. minced garlic

2 cups arborio rice

1 cup fresh Parmesan cheese, shredded

2 T. fresh rosemary leaves, diced

1 lb. large sea scallops

Salt and pepper to taste

PISTACHIO ROSEBUD COOKIES

These elegant cookies are as beautiful as they are delicious and simple. The buttery cookie topped with the chocolate, nuts, and rosebuds is a flavorful addition to any brunch, wedding shower, or afternoon tea party.

PREP TIME: 10 minutes › TOTAL TIME: 40 minutes › YIELD: 2 dozen cookies

INGREDIENTS

24 vanilla wafers

8 oz. of chocolate melting pieces (pure or almond bark)

¼ cup pistachios, shelled and roughly chopped

¼ cup organic rosebuds, roughly chopped

DIRECTIONS

Line a baking sheet with parchment paper and set it aside.

In a small saucepan, melt your chocolate on low heat, adding only a few cubes at a time, stirring constantly for approximately 5 minutes until smooth. When all the chocolate is completely melted, remove the pan from the heat.

Place the vanilla wafers right next to your pan, close to the lined baking sheet and the chopped nuts and rosebuds. Hold your pot of chocolate at an angle to create more depth, and dip each vanilla wafer in the chocolate, covering only half the cookie, then place it on the parchment paper and sprinkle the top with the nuts and flower buds, moving quickly before the chocolate dries. Gently press the pistachios and rose buds into the chocolate to ensure they are secured before the chocolate hardens. Let the cookies set up at room temperature for 30 minutes before serving.

MELON AND CUCUMBER BURRATA SALAD

As the temperatures rise, a fresh and light salad is always welcome. The crisp cucumber slices pair wonderfully with the melon. Burrata cheese has a mozzarella-like exterior, but the inside is a gooey mixture of cream and small cheese curds. The balsamic topping brings all these flavors together. This is a wonderful brunch or shower dish.

PREP TIME: 15 minutes > TOTAL TIME: 15 minutes > YIELD: 8 Servings

DIRECTIONS

Add the cucumber slices to a plate, leaving the center empty. Place the burrata in the center and layer the melon cubes and balls over the cucumber. Drizzle balsamic vinegar or balsamic glaze over the entire dish and sprinkle with fresh oregano leaves and a dash of salt. Chill and serve cold.

INGREDIENTS

1 cucumber, sliced in rounds

1 cup cantaloupe, cubed

1 cup watermelon balls

1 (8 oz.) ball of burrata cheese

Bundle of fresh oregano

1 T. balsamic glaze or balsamic vinegar

Salt to taste

WRANGLER CLUB WITH GARLIC AIOLI

Chicken thighs are one of the most affordable meals around and a delicious addition to any barbecue gathering. We've served the thighs as a stand-alone main course. However, when the boneless smoked chicken is added to a toasted bun and slathered with garlic aioli, onion strings, and bacon, it makes for a wonderful club sandwich.

PREP TIME: 20 minutes > TOTAL TIME: 6 hours > YIELD: 6 Servings

DIRECTIONS

Rinse the chicken and remove the bone from the underside: Place the thigh skin side down, locate the bone, and use a sharp knife to slice down the entire length, cutting all the way around the bone to remove it and leaving the rest of the thigh intact.

Make brine by dissolving the kosher salt and sugar in the water. Brine the thighs for 1 hour in the fridge, then remove, pat dry, and cover with dry rub on both sides, using about half of the rub mixture. Return them to the fridge for another 3½ hours.

Meanwhile, prepare both sauces: To make the aioli sauce, whisk the ingredients in a small bowl until smooth and chill for 1 hour. Combine the BBQ sauce with the jam and set aside. Preheat the smoker to 375°F. After the thighs have rested, add the remaining dry rub to both sides of the chicken. Put the thighs on the smoker, skin up, for 30 minutes, then flip them skin down for the next 20 minutes. Coat the chicken with the jam and BBQ sauce mixture and return it to the smoker for an additional 15 minutes or until the internal temperature reaches 170°F.

Remove the chicken from the smoker and let sit for 5 minutes while you assemble the sandwiches. Slather the toasted bottom bun with aioli. Add the bacon, smoked chicken, 2 tablespoons of onion straws, and the bun top. Serve with your favorite condiments, lettuce, or pickles.

INGREDIENTS

6 chicken thighs, skin on

1 cup kosher salt

½ cup sugar

1 gallon water

3 T. dry rub (page 86), divided

3 T. your favorite BBQ sauce

3 T. strawberry jalapeño jam (page 181)

6 hamburger buns, toasted

12 slices bacon, cooked

1 cup crispy onion straws

AIOLI INGREDIENTS

½ cup olive oil mayonnaise

1 T. minced garlic

2 tsp. lemon juice

¼ tsp. Dijon mustard

⅛ tsp. salt

CHOCOLATE DIRT CUPCAKES

These dirt cupcakes are a hit with kids and even the adults. I enjoyed bringing this special treat to the kids' field day at school. The frosted chocolate cupcake is topped with Oreo cookie crumbs and an edible flower. Serve the cupcake in a terra-cotta pot for a fun party treat.

PREP TIME: 15 minutes > TOTAL TIME: 1 hour, 5 minutes > YIELD: 12 Servings

INGREDIENTS

4 T. butter

¼ cup vegetable oil

½ cup water

1 cup flour

1 cup sugar

¼ cup plus 2 T. unsweetened cocoa powder

1 tsp. baking soda

¼ tsp. salt

1 tsp. instant coffee dissolved in 1 tsp. hot water

1 large egg

¼ cup buttermilk

1 tsp. vanilla extract

TOPPING INGREDIENTS

12 Oreo cookies

12 edible flowers

6 T. butter, softened

2⅓ cups powdered sugar

¾ cup unsweetened cocoa powder

⅓ cup whole milk

2 tsp. vanilla extract

¼ tsp. salt

DIRECTIONS

Preheat the oven to 350°F. Line a 12-cup muffin tin with paper liners.

In a medium saucepan, melt the butter with the vegetable oil and water over low heat. In a large bowl, sift the flour with the sugar, cocoa powder, baking soda, and salt. Add the melted butter mixture and beat with a mixer at low speed until smooth. Add the instant coffee mixture and egg and beat until incorporated. Then add the buttermilk and vanilla and beat until smooth, scraping the bottom and side of the bowl. Pour the batter into the lined muffin tins, filling them about three-fourths full.

Bake the cupcakes for about 25 minutes or until they are springy and a toothpick inserted in the center comes out clean. Let the cupcakes cool slightly, then transfer them out onto a rack to cool completely while you make the topping.

Place the Oreo cookies in a Ziploc bag and crush them with a rolling pin. Set aside.

Wash the edible flowers and remove the stems. Set aside.

Make the frosting: Blend the remainder of the topping ingredients in a mixer for 2 minutes on medium speed. Frost the cupcakes and then place them in small terra-cotta pots. Sprinkle the tops with the Oreo crumbs and add an edible flower to each cupcake.

SWEET STRAWBERRY SUN TEA

I grew up with a sun tea jar on our back deck at all times. This nostalgic drink is simple to make using the sun's rays to do the brewing. Adding a fruit-based simple syrup is our favorite way to make this classic sweet tea.

PREP TIME: 15 minutes > **TOTAL TIME: 4 hours, 15 minutes** > **YIELD: 8 Servings**

DIRECTIONS

Fill a large glass container with 8 cups of the water. Add the tea bags into the water. Securely cover with a lid or plastic wrap. Let it sit in direct sunlight for 4 hours. While your tea is brewing, you can make your stovetop strawberry simple syrup: Wash the berries and remove the stems, cut them into quarters, and add them to a small pot with 1 cup of water and the sugar. Bring the mixture to a boil, stirring continuously. Boil for 3 to 5 minutes, remove from heat, strain the strawberries, and let the syrup cool. When the sun tea is done brewing, bring it inside and add the simple syrup. Stir well until fully combined. Chill for 1 hour and serve over ice.

INGREDIENTS

9 cups water

8 black tea bags

3 cups fresh strawberries

1 cup sugar

Ice cubes

CREAM CHEESE CORN

Cream cheese corn is not to be mistaken for creamed corn—goodness, no! This is a hundred times better and is my daughter's all-time favorite dish. It seems strange for a teen girl to request corn, but it's that good. The herbs, cream cheese, and heavy cream make for a delicious sauce for the classic corn side dish.

PREP TIME: 15 minutes > TOTAL TIME: 50 minutes > YIELD: 8 Servings

DIRECTIONS

Preheat the oven to 350°F. Grease a baking dish and add cubes of cream cheese. Add the corn, heavy whipping cream, and smoked paprika into baking dish. Sprinkle herbs on top and bake for 20 minutes. Remove the dish and stir until all the cream cheese is evenly distributed. Bake for an additional 15 minutes.

INGREDIENTS

8 oz. cream cheese

8 cups corn cut off the cob (frozen or canned is also fine)

1 cup heavy whipping cream

1 tsp. smoked paprika

½ cup fresh parsley or oregano

PRESSED-FLOWER SUGAR COOKIES

Pressed flowers are all the rage, so why not add them to a delicious sugar cookie? This recipe works with various edible flowers, such as chamomile, calendula, violas, and pansies. A sprinkle of sugar on top will make these pressed-flower cookies the perfect addition to your afternoon tea.

PREP TIME: 20 minutes > TOTAL TIME: 2 hours, 40 minutes > YIELD: 3 dozen cookies

DIRECTIONS

Preheat the oven to 350°F. Combine the butter, sugar, and salt in a mixing bowl and then stir in the egg yolks and vanilla. With the mixer and paddle attachment on low speed, add the flour 1 cup at a time. The dough should form a ball. Place the dough ball on a sheet of lightly floured parchment paper and roll to a ⅓-inch thickness. Stamp out your cookies with a 2- or 3-inch cookie cutter, rerolling the scraps and cutting out more cookies.

Arrange the cookies on a parchment-lined baking sheet, leaving ¼ inch between cookies. Bake for about 9 minutes until the edges are golden brown.

While the cookies bake, remove the stems and leaves from the flowers and lay them on a paper towel. Immediately upon removing the cookies from the oven, place the edible flowers onto the cookies, gently patting them down to ensure they stick.

Layer a piece of parchment paper and then an empty cookie sheet on top of the cookies and lightly press for 1 to 2 minutes to help flatten the flowers into the cookies as they cool. Remove the top pan and parchment paper and sprinkle with sugar.

INGREDIENTS

1 cup edible flowers

1½ cups butter, softened

1⅓ cups sugar, plus more for sprinkling

1 tsp. salt

3 egg yolks

2 T. pure vanilla extract

4 cups all-purpose flour

Summer

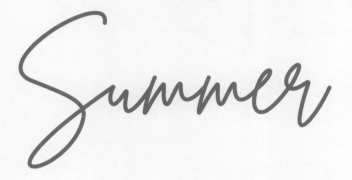

The bright rays of summer sunshine cascade across the gardens, inspiring growth and joy at the Grace-Filled Homestead. Cool mornings spent working in the garden give way to warm afternoons enjoying giggling kids running through the sprinkler and washing sticky popsicle hands.

Summer is barbecue season, and no one does it better than people of the Midwest, specifically our hometown of Kansas City. Every gathering has a billowing smoker, a blazing grill, or the familiar smell of classic charcoal briquets filling the air. It's potluck season where everyone brings a side dish or a fresh-fruit-inspired dessert. The volleyball net is up, and it's time for a serious competition. Remember, don't be a sore loser.

Baby spring chicks are now old enough to start laying their first rainbow-colored eggs. It's a gift to watch the baby goats transition to adventurous stinkers jumping on every bench and surface they come across. Midsummer goat snuggles at bedtime are our favorite, with a leafy snack from the garden for them and a magical lightshow from the dancing fireflies for us.

The bees are gathering their nourishment from the floral blooms, and the sweet honey flows into mason jars. Some of that harvested honey makes it into our sweet tea that is sipped as we relax on the front porch swing to savor the long summer days.

It's time for eating fresh tomatoes from the garden, foraging edible wildflowers from the field, and preserving produce with jams and canning. We can finally enjoy all the hard work of the past seasons. So let's take a stroll down the sunflower-lined path and soak up all God's simple pleasures and seasonal flavors. At last, summer!

BANANA FLAPJACKS WITH WILDFLOWER COMPOUND BUTTER

Sweet banana pancakes are a treat for any weekend breakfast. This wildflower compound butter has a touch of sweet local honey and is a fresh, flavorful addition to this dish. The scrumptious flapjacks pair wonderfully with the edible flowers, and when covered in syrup, they will make your taste buds sing.

PREP TIME: 15 minutes > TOTAL TIME: 35 minutes > YIELD: 8 Servings

DIRECTIONS

Start by making the compound butter so it can set up: Separate the petals of the flowers and remove any stalks. Chop the blooms and rosemary to a uniform size. Lay a rectangular piece of parchment paper on a clean, dry flat surface. Sprinkle half of the edible flowers and herbs on the paper. Combine the butter and honey, then spread the mixture gently on the flowers and herbs. Level it with the flat side of a knife, making a 6 x 6-inch square.

Sprinkle the other half of the flowers and herbs on top of the honey butter. If the honey butter is very soft, keep it (still on the paper) in the fridge for 5 minutes to firm up a bit. Use a knife to lift one edge of the butter from the paper and roll it. Wrap the roll of butter in the paper and twist the ends. Place it in the fridge to chill.

Now for the pancakes: In a bowl, use a fork to mash the peeled bananas. Mix in all the other ingredients except the melted butter, and stir to form a smooth, thick batter. Heat a skillet over medium heat. Once the cooking surface is hot, lightly grease the pan with a small amount of the melted butter and add the pancake batter, using ⅓ cup per pancake. Cook the first side until the tops of the pancakes begin to bubble. Flip and cook until cooked through. Repeat this process until all your batter is cooked.

Remove the cold butter roll from the refrigerator. Unwrap the butter log, press in a couple of edible flowers on the top for garnish, and slice it into small rounds.

Plate your banana flapjacks and top them with the compound butter rounds and pure maple syrup.

INGREDIENTS

2 large overly ripe bananas

1 cup flour

1 T. sugar

2 tsp. baking powder

½ tsp. salt

2 eggs

3 T. milk

1 tsp. vanilla extract

2 T. butter, melted, to coat pan

BUTTER INGREDIENTS

1 cup butter, softened

1 tsp. honey

1 tsp. fresh rosemary, chopped

2 T. edible flowers, chopped, plus 5 whole flowers for garnish

BASIL PESTO PASTA

Fresh basil is a summer treat right out of the herb garden. Our favorite way to enjoy it is in a pesto sauce. We use pesto in many recipes, and when it's mixed with a fettuccini pasta and served with crusty garlic bread, it makes a scrumptious meal. This is also a lovely summer side dish to offer alongside many different entrees.

PREP TIME: 5 minutes › **TOTAL TIME:** 25 minutes › **YIELD:** 6 Servings

INGREDIENTS

½ cup pine nuts or cashews

2 cups packed fresh basil leaves

¾ cup grated Parmesan cheese

1 T. lemon juice

2 tsp. minced garlic

½ tsp. salt

1 cup olive oil

1 lb. fettuccini pasta

DIRECTIONS

Toast the nuts in a skillet over medium heat for 5 minutes. Remove them from the heat and allow them to cool. In a food processor, add the basil, nuts, cheese, lemon juice, garlic, and salt. With the processor running, drizzle in the olive oil and continue processing until smooth. Cook the pasta in boiling water for approximately 12 minutes or to desired texture. Reserve ⅓ cup of the pasta-cooking water before draining. Place the drained, cooked pasta in a serving dish and add the pesto sauce to the warm pasta with splashes of the pasta water until you reach your desired consistency. Serve with a crusty garlic bread.

BEET AND ARUGULA SALAD WITH BACON-WRAPPED GOAT CHEESE

Beets and arugula are a delicious summer duet. This salad is topped with bacon-wrapped goat cheese and crunchy pistachios. It is tossed in a simple balsamic vinaigrette.

PREP TIME: 30 minutes > TOTAL TIME: 1 hour > YIELD: 6 Servings

DIRECTIONS

Cut the goat cheese log into 6 equally sized rounds. Wrap each goat cheese cylinder with 1 piece of bacon and secure with a toothpick if needed. Place the rounds on a tray in the freezer for 30 minutes.

Preheat the oven to 350°F. Place chilled goat cheese rounds on a parchment-lined pan and bake for about 20 minutes or until the bacon is cooked and crispy.

To make the dressing, whisk the olive oil, vinegar, mustard, and salt together. In a large bowl toss the arugula, beets, pistachios, and radishes with the dressing. Serve with a bacon-wrapped goat cheese round.

INGREDIENTS

6 oz. goat cheese

6 slices bacon

3 T. olive oil

2 T. balsamic vinegar

1 tsp. stone ground mustard

¼ tsp. salt

6 cups arugula

2 cups pickled or steamed beets, chopped into 1-inch chunks

½ cup pistachios, roughly chopped

3 radishes, sliced

HERB-STUFFED CORNISH HENS

Cornish hens are a fun addition to serve at a summer gathering. There is something special about having your own mini roasted bird. The infused buttery herb flavors are a delight to kids and adults alike. For a delicious meal, serve with a salad of mixed greens topped with strawberries, pecans, blue cheese crumbles, and a raspberry vinaigrette.

PREP TIME: 15 minutes > TOTAL TIME: 1 hour, 30 minutes > YIELD: 4 Servings

DIRECTIONS

Preheat the oven to 375°F. Gently lift the skin from the hen breasts and place 1 pat of butter under the skin of each. Place 2 more pats inside the cavity, using four pats per bird. Into each cavity, place a lemon wedge, 2 chopped green onions, one bay leaf, and one sprig of thyme. Tuck the wings under the hens and tie the legs together. Place them in a greased roasting pan.

Combine the melted butter, oil, minced garlic, and lemon juice. Brush half the mixture on the outside of the hens, then sprinkle with salt and pepper. Bake for 30 minutes. Remove the hens from oven and brush the rest of the melted butter mixture on the hens. Bake for an additional 45 minutes or until the internal temperature of the thigh reaches 170°F.

Serve with a mixed greens salad. Enjoy!

INGREDIENTS

4 Cornish game hens

1 stick (8 oz.) butter, cut into 16 pats

1 lemon, cut in wedges

8 green onions, roughly chopped

4 sprigs thyme

4 bay leaves

4 T. butter, melted

4 T. olive oil

2 tsp. minced garlic

4 T. lemon juice

2 tsp. kosher salt

½ tsp. ground pepper

SWEET ZUCCHINI SCONES WITH APRICOT COMPOTE

This sweet scone recipe is our delicious take on zucchini bread. The small bites of glazed goodness pair wonderfully with the apricot compote. Compote is very similar to jam, but it's made without sugar or pectin, so it's considered a bit healthier. This is a great recipe for your summer brunch or afternoon tea.

PREP TIME: 10 minutes > TOTAL TIME: 35 minutes > YIELD: 6 Servings

DIRECTIONS

Preheat the oven to 350°F. Place the sour cream in a bowl and mix in the baking soda. In another mixing bowl, whisk together the flour, sugar, baking powder, and salt. Shred the cold butter and use a pastry blender to cut it into the flour mixture until the butter is broken into pea-sized morsels in the flour. Beat the egg and mix it into the sour cream, then add in the vanilla.

Stir the sour cream mixture into the dry mixture, working it in. The dough can be a bit dry. If you use your hands to combine it, avoid overworking the dough, so the heat of your hands doesn't melt the butter. You want your scone dough to be a bit dry. When the dough is combined, mix in the zucchini.

Place the dough onto a floured surface, patting it into a 6-inch circle, 1 inch thick. Cut the circle into 12 equal triangles. Place the scones 1 inch apart on a parchment-lined baking sheet and bake for 20 to 25 minutes until browned nicely on the bottom and slightly on the top.

Prepare the fruit compote and glaze while your scones are baking: First, add the apricots to a small saucepan with the honey and vanilla, stirring over medium heat until it comes to a boil. Reduce the heat to low and simmer for 10 minutes, then remove from the heat and allow the compote to cool. For the glaze, combine the powdered sugar and just enough lemon juice to reach a thin, spreadable consistency.

Once the scones are baked and cooled, drizzle them with glaze and serve with the apricot compote. Enjoy!

INGREDIENTS
½ cup sour cream

½ tsp. baking soda

1½ cups flour

½ cup sugar

1 tsp. baking powder

½ tsp. salt

½ cup butter, cold

1 egg

¼ tsp. vanilla extract

¼ cup finely shredded zucchini

COMPOTE INGREDIENTS
3 ripe apricots, pitted, unpeeled, and diced

2 T. honey

1 tsp. vanilla extract

GLAZE INGREDIENTS
2 cups powdered sugar

3 tablespoons lemon juice

SIMPLE FRUIT JAM

Fruit jam is one of the simple pleasures in life, especially when it's slathered over a warm biscuit. It's easier than you think to make your own, whether you enjoy peach, blueberry, or strawberry. Your ingredients can be local in-season fruit, or you can combine berries for a unique masterpiece. Of course, frozen berries are a great option during the rest of the year.

PREP TIME: 25 minutes > **TOTAL TIME: 24 hours** > **YIELD: 4 (16 oz.) jars of jam**

INGREDIENTS

5 cups fruit, crushed
(peeled if you prefer)

¼ cup lemon juice

1 (1.75 oz.) box of
powdered fruit pectin

7 cups white sugar

DIRECTIONS

Wash canning jars and lids in hot, soapy water, rinse well, and dry. Place the fruit, lemon juice, and pectin into a large saucepan and bring to a full boil over high heat. Once the fruit is boiling, stir in the sugar until dissolved, return to a full boil, and cook for 1 minute. Ladle the hot jam into jars and cover tightly with lids. Allow the jam to sit at room temperature for 24 hours to set, then refrigerate for up to a month.

CUCUMBER LIMEADE SPRITZERS

Limeade is one of our treasured summer drinks. The refreshing lime and cucumber flavors go wonderfully with the fizzy soda water. The herbed sugar rim makes this concoction a fabulous addition to any gathering.

PREP TIME: 10 minutes > TOTAL TIME: 35 minutes > YIELD: 6 Servings

DIRECTIONS

In a saucepan set to high heat, bring the water and ¾ cup of the sugar to a boil to make the simple syrup base, stirring until the sugar dissolves. Remove from heat. Stir in ¼ cup of the mint leaves and steep for 10 minutes. Strain the syrup and discard the solids. Cool the syrup completely, approximately 15 minutes.

Use a mortar and pestle (or a wooden spoon and a small bowl) to muddle and smash the chopped cucumber to release the juice. Combine the smashed cucumber with the lime juice and stir until smooth. In a large pitcher, stir together the simple syrup, cucumber-lime mixture, and club soda.

To sugar the rims of your glasses, finely chop 1 teaspoon of mint and combine it on a small plate with the lime zest and the final ¼ cup of sugar. Moisten the rim of each glass with a lime wedge. Press the glass rim down gently into the mint sugar mixture, twisting it until it is evenly coated. Fill the glasses with ice and pour in the spritzer. Garnish with mint sprigs, lime, and cucumber slices.

INGREDIENTS

½ cup water

1 cup sugar, divided

¼ cup plus 1 tsp. fresh mint leaves

½ cup cucumber, peeled and finely chopped

½ cup fresh lime juice

6 cups club soda

1 tsp. lime zest

Mint leaves, lime, and cucumber slices for garnish

RASPBERRY LEMONADE BLOOM POPSICLES

Fruity popsicles have always been a fun way to beat the summer heat. These tart lemonade popsicles are filled with sweet raspberries, additional fruit, and edible blooms. They are so refreshing, you will want another one.

PREP TIME: 15 minutes > TOTAL TIME: 8 hours > YIELD: 8 Servings

DIRECTIONS

Add half the raspberries, half the lemon juice, and the sugar to a blender. Blend the mixture until it is smooth and the sugar has completely dissolved, about 3 minutes. Strain the mixture into a pitcher with a fine mesh strainer to separate the raspberries seeds and pulp from the juice. Add the water and the rest of the lemon juice into the pitcher and stir until combined. Place the flowers, remaining raspberries, and additional fruit into popsicle molds. Pour in the raspberry lemonade, leaving about ¼ inch at the top of each mold to allow for expansion. If the flowers and fruit remain at the top, use a popsicle stick to push them farther down into the mold. Place sticks into the molds and freeze overnight. To remove the popsicles from the molds, run them under room-temperature water until they loosen.

INGREDIENTS

1 cup fresh raspberries, divided

1 cup fresh squeezed lemon juice, divided

1¼ cup sugar

6 cups water

½ cup additional fruit in small pieces (we used kiwis)

½ cup edible flowers

SHRIMP BOIL WITH CORN AND POTATOES

A one-pot shrimp boil is a wonderful way to feed a large gathering of friends and family. It makes for a beautiful table display since your food is the centerpiece, as it should be. The scrumptious lemon butter and cheddar-chive biscuits (next recipe) are the perfect additions to this table full of goodness!

PREP TIME: 10 minutes › TOTAL TIME: 35 minutes › YIELD: 12 Servings

INGREDIENTS

1¼ gallons water

4 lemons, halved

2 T. minced garlic

6 oz. Old Bay Seasoning

2 lb. baby red potatoes, halved

8 ears corn, cut in thirds

2 lb. jumbo shrimp, deveined

BUTTER INGREDIENTS

1 cup butter, melted

1 T. minced garlic

½ cup broth from cooking shrimp

Juice and zest of 1 lemon

DIRECTIONS

Add the water, lemon, and garlic to a large stock pot. Stir in Old Bay Seasoning. Cover and bring to a boil over medium heat. Add in the potatoes and cook for 10 minutes. Add in the corn and continue cooking at a simmer for another 5 minutes. Add in the shrimp and cook for 2 to 3 minutes until the shrimp turn pink. Remove the potatoes, corn, and shrimp from the broth using a large slotted spoon and place them in a large bowl. To make the lemon butter, whisk together the melted butter, garlic, lemon juice, and broth in a small bowl, and then add the lemon zest. Sprinkle additional Old Bay Seasoning into the butter as desired.

To serve this, we place butcher paper down the center of the table as a runner and pour the shrimp, potatoes, and corn across the table. Serve with the lemon butter and cheddar chive biscuits (page 81).

CHEDDAR CHIVE BISCUITS

Cheddar Chive Biscuits are a delicious addition to any meal, especially with a summer seafood spread. This flaky biscuit is filled with cheesy goodness and herbed flavor.

PREP TIME: 15 minutes › TOTAL TIME: 30 minutes › YIELD: 8 Servings

DIRECTIONS

Preheat the oven to 425°F. Line a baking sheet with parchment paper.

Place the buttermilk in the freezer for 15 minutes while prepping the other ingredients. In a large bowl, whisk the flour, baking powder, sugar, salt, and baking soda. Add the cheese and chives into the flour mixture. After the buttermilk has been chilled, combine it with the melted butter. Stir the butter in with a fork until it forms small clumps. Add the buttermilk mixture to the dry ingredients and stir just until all the flour is incorporated and the batter pulls away from the sides of the bowl. The dough should be stiff and not super wet. If the dough is wet, add more flour 1 tablespoon at a time.

Generously spread flour over your work surface. Place the biscuit dough onto the prepared work surface and turn it to coat each surface of the dough with flour. Knead it on the counter for 1 minute, then pat it into a 6-inch square that is about 2 inches high. Cut the biscuits with a 2-inch biscuit cutter. Place the biscuits on the prepared baking sheet and knead the scraps a few times until they hold together. Pat out the remaining dough and cut more biscuits. Transfer the last biscuits to the sheet pan, spacing about 1½ inches apart. Bake until the tops are a medium golden brown, about 8 to 10 minutes. Remove from oven. Brush the tops of the hot biscuits with the remaining tablespoon of melted butter. Sprinkle with more finely chopped fresh chives. Serve and enjoy!

INGREDIENTS

1 cup buttermilk

2 cups flour, plus more for kneading

2 teaspoons baking powder

1 tsp. sugar

¾ tsp. salt

½ tsp. baking soda

1¾ cups finely shredded cheddar cheese

¼ cup fresh chives, finely chopped

½ cup melted butter, plus 1 T. for brushing

BLUEBERRY SMOOTHIE BOWL

We love smoothie bowls at the Grace-Filled Homestead. Inspired by the delicious acai berry bowls we enjoyed on a West Coast vacation, we adapted the recipe to include local and seasonal berries. The blueberry smoothie is packed with nutrients from the spirulina protein, nuts, fruit, and granola. The superfoods of blueberries and blue spirulina are fun and healthy additions to create a smoothie rich in protein, vitamins, minerals, and antioxidants.

PREP TIME: 5 minutes > TOTAL TIME: 5 minutes > YIELD: 4 Servings

DIRECTIONS

Add the frozen fruit, spirulina powder, and almond milk to a blender. Mix on high until smooth and creamy. Divide the smoothie evenly into 4 bowls and top with nuts, granola, and fresh fruit. Drizzle local honey over the top and garnish with edible flowers. Enjoy!

INGREDIENTS

½ cup frozen blueberries

1 cup frozen banana chunks

1 cup frozen mango chunks

1 tsp. blue spirulina powder or a scoop of your favorite protein powder

¾ cup vanilla almond milk

4 tsp. honey

Desired toppings, such as almonds, granola, fresh fruit, and edible flowers

SMOKED KANSAS CITY BBQ RIBS

Smoked ribs are the centerpiece of our family gatherings. In Kansas City, the barbecue capital of the world, every family member has their own favorite sauce. Debates about the topic are more heated and passionate than any political argument you've seen. Therefore, we serve our ribs dry and let our family and friends choose which sauce to add. We use a traditional smoker for this recipe, but we've added an optional grill method that is just as delicious!

PREP TIME: 30 minutes > TOTAL TIME: 6 hours > YIELD: 6 Servings

DIRECTIONS

Preheat the smoker to 225°F. Rinse the ribs and remove the silver skin membrane from the underside of the ribs. To do so, insert a butter knife just under the membrane and work your fingers through each section to pull it off. Generously spread Outlaw BBQ rub on both sides of the ribs. Rub it in thoroughly. Place the ribs in the smoker, meat side up. The smoking temperature should be between 200 and 250°F degrees. Cook for 3 hours. Remove the ribs, place them on a long sheet of heavy-duty foil, spray the ribs with apple juice, and then wrap them up and return the foil-wrapped ribs to the smoker for an additional 2 hours. Finish as described below.

ALTERNATIVE GRILL METHOD

If you prefer to use a grill instead of a smoker, place the apple juice and the liquid smoke in the bottom of a large foil roasting pan. Place the prepared ribs, with the rub on them, in the foil pan, meat side up so they hover over the juice mixture. Cover the top of the roasting pan with foil and place it on the preheated grill at 300°F for 1 hour. Check the ribs to ensure the apple juice mixture is evaporating and the ribs are becoming charred but not burnt. Adjust the temperature down a bit if needed. Cook for an additional hour.

TO FINISH

When the ribs are done, remove them from the smoker or grill and let them rest for an additional 30 minutes. If you would like to serve the ribs with the sauce on, paint both sides with your favorite sauce and cook an additional 15 minutes before letting them rest. Turn the rack over and slice between the bones. Enjoy!

INGREDIENTS

2 slabs of 3 lb. baby back ribs

¼ cup apple juice

1 cup Outlaw BBQ rub (page 86)

½ cup your favorite BBQ sauce

GRILL METHOD INGREDIENTS

1½ cup apple juice

1 T. liquid smoke

1 large foil roasting pan

OUTLAW BBQ RUB

The Outlaw BBQ Rub is a blend of sassy spices that we use on beef, pork, and chicken. It can be made in a bigger batch and stored for daily use. This Kansas City barbecue rub is what dreams are made of.

PREP TIME: 5 minutes > **TOTAL TIME: 5 minutes** > **YIELD: 10 Servings**

INGREDIENTS

1 T. cayenne pepper

3 T. smoked paprika

2 T. salt

2 tsp. garlic powder

1 tsp. mustard powder

1 tsp. onion powder

2 tsp. black pepper

½ cup brown sugar

DIRECTIONS

Combine all the ingredients and mix well. The barbecue rub will keep for up to 3 months stored in a cool, dry place.

CRUNCHY COLESLAW

This slaw recipe is on our family's regular meal rotation. It is always a hit at our barbecue cookouts as well as with our favorite Asian meals. We double the recipe because it's even better on day two.

PREP TIME: 15 minutes > TOTAL TIME: 1 hour, 15 minutes > YIELD: 8 Servings

DIRECTIONS

Place the cabbage in a large bowl. Crush the dry ramen noodles and add them to the cabbage. Mix in the sunflower seeds, sliced almonds, and green onions. In a separate bowl, whisk together the oil, vinegar, ramen seasoning packets, and sugar. Pour the dressing mixture over the coleslaw mix and toss until coated well. Cover the bowl and place it in the refrigerator for at least 1 hour.

INGREDIENTS

1 green cabbage, finely chopped

1 carrot, shredded

2 (3 oz.) bags chicken ramen with seasoning packet

½ cup shelled sunflower seeds

½ cup sliced almonds

8 stalks green onion, sliced

½ cup oil

⅓ cup white vinegar

½ cup sugar

STARS AND STRIPES CHOCOLATE CHEESECAKE

This patriotic dessert is adapted from Grandma's version of a dessert she called Robert Redford. It has a nutty butter-filled crust and layers of chocolate cheesecake. We add the fruit toppings for a holiday celebration to remember.

PREP TIME: 20 minutes > TOTAL TIME: 2 hours, 50 minutes > YIELD: 12 Servings

DIRECTIONS

Preheat the oven to 350°F. Lay the berries out on a paper towel and pat to dry off the excess liquid. Let them sit while you make the crust and filling.

Combine the flour, ½ cup of the butter, and the pecans. Press the mixture into the bottom of a 9 x 13-inch pan. Bake for 25 minutes or until golden brown, then allow it to cool. You can speed up the cooling time by placing the pan in the fridge or freezer.

Combine the cream cheese, sugar, and half the whipped cream until it is well mixed, then spread it evenly over the cooled crust.

Combine the chocolate and vanilla pudding mixes with the milk in a mixing bowl. Beat well for 2 minutes and allow it to rest to firm up for 5 minutes, then spread the pudding evenly over the cream-cheese filling.

Spread the remaining whipped cream over the pudding layer. Add a square of blueberries to the top left corner of the pan, then add stripes of raspberries. Chill for 2 hours before serving.

INGREDIENTS

1 cup flour

1 cup butter, softened and divided

1 cup chopped pecans

8 oz. cream cheese, softened

1 cup sugar

16 oz. whipped cream (homemade or thawed Cool Whip), divided

4 oz. instant chocolate pudding mix powder

4 oz. instant vanilla pudding mix powder

3 cups milk

1 cup blueberries

2 cups raspberries

MOLASSES BAKED BEANS

Baked beans are a staple at the barbecue gatherings in our neck of the woods. Our sweet molasses made-from-scratch recipe is filled with scrumptious maple bacon and smoky flavors. You can cook and serve it right out of the Crock-Pot.

PREP TIME: 30 minutes > TOTAL TIME: 16 hours > YIELD: 10 Servings

INGREDIENTS

3 cups dried navy beans, soaked overnight

24 slices maple bacon, chopped

1 onion, chopped

½ cup molasses

1 cup ketchup

1½ cups brown sugar

¼ cup maple syrup

2 tsp. salt

1 T. dry mustard

2 T. apple cider vinegar

1 cup apple juice

1 cup water

DIRECTIONS

To prepare the beans, rinse, check for debris, and soak overnight. Drain, then add fresh water to cover the beans. Bring to a boil, reduce heat, and simmer for 1 hour. Drain again.

Add half the bacon to the bottom of the slow cooker, and layer the beans and then the onions on top. Add the other half of the bacon to the top of the onions. Do not stir. Cover with the lid and turn on the cooker to low while you make the sauce.

In a small bowl, whisk together all the remaining ingredients, then pour the sauce over the bacon and bean layers. Once again, do not stir it. Replace the lid and cook for 6 hours on low.

After the 6 hours you can stir it to check for doneness. The sauce will be thick. If you would like the beans to be tenderer, cook for an additional hour.

PATRIOT PUNCH

We've been making this Independence Day punch since the kids were tiny, and they loved it. This red, white, and blue drink is a refreshing addition to your holiday gatherings. The layering is based on the sugar content of the drink. The red layer should have the highest sugar content to keep it separated from the blue. The white layer should have the least amount of sugar with additional ice. This is a fun drink that also can be made in individual glasses.

PREP TIME: 5 minutes > TOTAL TIME: 5 minutes > YIELD: 8 Servings

DIRECTIONS

Fill your drink container to the top with ice. Pour cold cranberry juice in until it fills about ⅓ of the container. Add the chilled blue sports drink, again filling another ⅓ of the glass or container. As you add the blue beverage, pour it slowly and directly on top of an ice cube so the ice cube will slow down the process of the liquids mixing with each other. Add crushed ice to the top of the container. The density of the crushed ice will help keep the diet soda from blending in to the blue and adds to the appearance of the white layer. Finally, add the diet lemon lime soda, filling up the glass or container to the top.

INGREDIENTS

Cranberry juice
(I use Ocean Spray), chilled

Blue sports drink
(I use Gatorade), chilled

Diet lemon lime soda
(I use Sprite), chilled

1 bag regular ice

½ bag crushed ice

Note: amounts needed will vary to fit your container

CHERRY DUMP COBBLER

Nothing says summertime more than a fruit cobbler. The tart cherries against the buttery cobbler crust are delicious. This cobbler is so simple to make. Serve this warm with vanilla ice cream.

PREP TIME: 15 minutes > TOTAL TIME: 1 hour, 30 minutes > YIELD: 12 Servings

DIRECTIONS

Preheat the oven to 350°F. Spray a 13 x 9-inch baking dish with cooking spray. Spread the cherry pie filling in the baking dish. Top the fruit layer with the dry cake mix, distributing it evenly across the top. Cut the butter into thin pats by cutting each stick in half and then in half again, then cutting 6 more pats per section. This gives you 24 pats of butter per stick. Cover the dry cake mixture with the butter pats. Bake for 1 hour or until the top is golden brown. Cool the cobbler for 15 minutes before serving with vanilla ice cream.

INGREDIENTS

60 oz. canned cherry pie filling

1 yellow cake mix

2 sticks butter

RATTLESNAKE CHICKEN PASTA

This spicy pasta dish is easy to make and hearty enough to leave you full. The rotisserie chicken, pasta, and sassy alfredo sauce combine for a delicious main course your friends and family will love.

PREP TIME: 20 minutes > TOTAL TIME: 35 minutes > YIELD: 6 Servings

DIRECTIONS

Cook the pasta by boiling over medium heat for 12 minutes, then drain and set aside. Meanwhile, remove the roasted chicken from the bone and cut it into 1-inch chunks, leaving the skin on for flavor.

In a large skillet, melt the butter over medium heat. Add the onion and garlic, then stir for 3 minutes. Remove the seeds from the bell peppers and jalapeños. Slice the bell peppers into strips and the jalapeños into rounds. Add the flour to the skillet mixture and stir to make a roux. Slowly add the milk, stirring continuously to combine thoroughly. Add the bell peppers and jalapeños. Next, stir in the heavy cream. Bring to a simmer for 3 minutes and then add the Parmesan cheese. Stir for an additional 7 minutes. Fold in the pasta and serve immediately.

INGREDIENTS

1 lb. penne pasta

1 rotisserie chicken

4 T. butter

1 cup chopped onion

2 tsp. minced garlic

2 bell peppers

3 jalapeños

⅓ cup flour

3 cups milk

1 cup heavy whipping cream

1½ cups Parmesan cheese, shredded

1 tsp. salt

½ tsp. pepper

LADYBUG CAPRESE MINI-SALAD

Caprese salad has always been a favorite at the Grace-Filled Homestead. This fun twist on a classic will be sure to bring a smile to anyone's face. We love our live ladybugs in the garden and these mozzarella treats on our buffet table.

PREP TIME: 10 minutes > TOTAL TIME: 30 minutes > YIELD: 12 servings

DIRECTIONS

Place mozzarella slices on a serving dish as the base for your appetizer. Layer one basil leaf on each cheese slice. Cut the cherry tomatoes in half and then make an additional slice lengthwise halfway up, separating the wings. Place a tomato half, cut side down, on each herb leaf. After cutting the olives in half, position half an olive at the end of each tomato. Dip a toothpick into the balsamic glaze and place a few dots on the tomato. Chill for 20 minutes before serving.

INGREDIENTS

2 large (8 oz.)
mozzarella balls, sliced

12 basil leaves

6 cherry tomatoes

6 large black olives

1 T. balsamic glaze

NANNIE'S PINEAPPLE UPSIDE-DOWN CAKE

This vintage dessert was a favorite at every gathering in the '70s and '80s, and for good reason. Nannie's recipe was the best pineapple upside-down cake in the neighborhood, with the caramelized brown sugar, fruit topping, and buttery cake.

PREP TIME: 15 minutes › TOTAL TIME: 45 minutes › YIELD: 8 Servings

INGREDIENTS

½ cup salted butter, softened

¾ cup sugar

2 eggs

1 cup milk

1 tsp. vanilla extract

1½ cups flour

1½ tsp. baking powder

¼ tsp. salt

TOPPING INGREDIENTS

¼ cup salted butter, melted

½ cup brown sugar

14 pineapple slices, patted dry

Maraschino cherries

DIRECTIONS

Preheat the oven to 350°F. The topping ingredients will go in the bottom of the pan. Pour the melted butter into 2 (8-inch) round cake pans or a 9 x 13-inch cake pan. Be sure to coat the sides as well. Sprinkle brown sugar evenly over the butter. Arrange pineapple slices over the bottom of the pan. Place cherries in the center of the pineapple rings. Set aside.

To prepare the cake, beat the butter and sugar together. Add the eggs, milk, and vanilla and continue to beat until combined. In a separate bowl, whisk together the flour, baking powder, and salt. Carefully stir the wet ingredients into the dry ingredients. Pour the batter evenly over the prepared cake pan and pineapple-cherry layer. Bake for 25 to 30 minutes. Allow the cake to cool for 15 minutes and then carefully invert it onto a serving dish. If you are using two round pans, invert the second cake directly on top of the first cake. Enjoy!

FRIED GREEN TOMATOES WITH FIRECRACKER RÉMOULADE

Fried green tomatoes are a farm-fresh tradition. They are crispy on the outside and served with a spicy rémoulade sauce for dipping. They are such a treat to look forward to every summer.

PREP TIME: 10 minutes > TOTAL TIME: 30 minutes > YIELD: 6 Servings

DIRECTIONS

To make the rémoulade, combine the mayonnaise, sour cream, hot sauce, mustard, garlic, and Cajun seasoning. Refrigerate while you are frying the tomatoes.

Slice unpeeled tomatoes ½ inch thick. Sprinkle both sides of the slices with salt, then let the tomatoes sit for 5 minutes on paper towels to draw out some liquid.

Preheat the oil in a skillet on medium heat.

Meanwhile, combine the flour, Cajun seasoning, and cornmeal in a shallow bowl. Whisk the buttermilk and egg together in a separate bowl. Blot the juices off the tomatoes with a paper towel, and dip them into the egg mixture and then into the flour mixture. Fry the coated tomatoes in the hot oil. Work in batches, frying tomatoes for approximately 4 to 5 minutes on each side or until they are golden brown. Drain the fried tomatoes on a rack lined with paper towels. Serve with Firecracker Rémoulade.

INGREDIENTS

4 large green tomatoes

1 tsp. salt

¾ cup flour

1 T. Cajun seasoning

½ cup cornmeal

½ cup buttermilk

1 large egg

½ cup vegetable oil for frying

1 T. red pepper flakes for garnish

RÉMOULADE INGREDIENTS

½ cup mayonnaise

½ cup sour cream

4 T. hot sauce

2 T. spicy brown mustard

1 tsp. minced garlic

2 tsp. Cajun seasoning

BBQ PULLED PORK AND CHEESY GRITS

Cheesy grits are a way of life in our hometown. This comfort food is taken to the next level as a main dish with a pulled pork topping that is packed with flavor.

PREP TIME: 10 minutes > TOTAL TIME: 35 minutes > YIELD: 6 Servings

DIRECTIONS

In a medium saucepan, bring the chicken broth to a boil. Add the garlic and slowly stir in the grits. Reduce the heat to medium low and cook, stirring frequently, until the grits are tender, about 20 minutes. Remove the saucepan from the heat and stir in the cheese, butter, and cream. Season with salt and pepper.

To make the pork topping, add the prepared pulled pork to a saucepan with the Heinz 57 and BBQ rub. Stir continuously over low heat for 5 minutes. Plate the warm grits individually with even amounts of pork topping. Enjoy!

NOTE: If you are unable to locate old-fashioned grits, you can substitute quick grits. Reduce your cooking time from 20 minutes to 5 minutes.

INGREDIENTS
4 cups chicken broth

½ tsp. garlic minced

1 cup old-fashioned grits

1½ cups shredded white cheddar cheese

¼ cup butter

2 T. heavy cream

Salt and pepper to taste

TOPPING INGREDIENTS
2 cups pulled pork (page 39)

½ cup Heinz 57 sauce

2 tsp. Outlaw BBQ rub (page 86)

GRILLED PEACHES WITH VANILLA BEAN ICE CREAM

Grilled peaches are a summertime treat at the Grace-Filled Homestead. Our recipe is delicious and a bit sassy, adding the spicy Hot Honey. This is a refreshing ending to any outdoor barbecue gathering.

PREP TIME: 5 minutes › TOTAL TIME: 15 minutes › YIELD: 8 Servings

DIRECTIONS

Preheat the grill on medium heat. Cut the peaches in half and remove the pits, leaving the skin on. Using extra ripe peaches will allow the seed to be removed easily. Brush the cut side of the peaches with melted butter and place them on the hot grill, cut side down. Do not move for 4 minutes to ensure grill marks are made. Turn the peaches over and place over indirect heat for an additional 4 minutes. Place the grilled peaches on individual plates and top with a scoop of vanilla bean ice cream and a drizzle of Hot Honey.

INGREDIENTS

4 peaches

2 T. melted butter

8 scoops of vanilla bean ice cream (about 1 quart)

¼ cup Hot Honey (page 215)

OUTLAW BEEF BRISKET

Kansas City is the barbecue capital of the world, and beef brisket is always the darling of the show. Our recipe is packed with flavorful juices and a smoky rub. This brisket takes all day long to smoke, but it's worth the wait.

PREP TIME: 10 minutes › TOTAL TIME: 12 hours › YIELD: 12 Servings

INGREDIENTS

12 lb. prime beef brisket, untrimmed

1 cup apple juice

1 ½ cups Outlaw BBQ rub (page 86)

DIRECTIONS

Preheat the smoker to 225°F. Place the meat fat side down and remove the silver skin (the shiny thin membrane). Turn over the brisket and trim the fat down to ¼ inch. Coat the entire brisket with the dry rub. Work it in generously. Place the meat fat side up on the smoker. Smoke until the internal temperature reaches 160°F, approximately 8 hours. Roll out a double thick piece of foil and place the meat on the foil. Spray a generous amount of apple juice on the meat and then wrap it tightly in the foil. Place the brisket back on the smoker until the internal temperature reaches 202°F (approximately 2 to 3 hours). Pull it off the smoker and wrap the foil-wrapped brisket in a towel. Place it inside an empty cooler at room temperature to rest for 2 hours with the lid shut. This will keep it warm and allow the juices to settle. Pull the brisket out of the cooler, unwrap it, and slice it against the grain on a cutting board. Serve it with your favorite sauce. Enjoy!

Fall

As the temperature begins to drop and the leaves turn brilliant autumn colors, we welcome the harvest season. At the Grace-Filled Homestead, this is when we throw on cozy flannel shirts, light the campfire, and spend time with our loved ones. We enjoy spice-filled pastries, cast-iron-skillet comfort foods, and game-day snacks with our closest friends and family.

I look forward to the first brisk morning of fall, when I can light the fireplace and savor a mug of warm goodness beside it. During this season, we layer our sweaters and enjoy the outdoors every chance we get. Each fall is marked with an annual day trip to a pumpkin patch located a few towns north of ours. We first stop at the apple orchard farmstand for delicious hot apple fritters covered in powdered sugar. Then we head across the lane to pick our pumpkins and love on the farm animals. This family tradition holds a special place in our hearts.

A simple farm-to-table dinner with our closest friends and family is a joyful way to celebrate the harvest and the hard work put in during the spring and summer months. Dining beneath twinkle lights and a canopy of stars can turn any autumn farmhouse dinner into a magical evening.

Our Thanksgiving gathering is one of the highlights of our year at the Grace-Filled Homestead. It is beautiful and chaotic with adorable little ones running around, friends and family catching up, and a feast made for royalty. Even in the most difficult of years, autumn ushers in a season of giving thanks, reflecting on God's goodness, and expressing gratitude for all our blessings.

PUMPKIN SPICE MUFFINS

By September my daughter is excited for pumpkin spice season. We celebrate its arrival with a pumpkin spice muffin and a trip to the local coffee house. The crumble topping on this muffin is delicious, especially when paired with the nutmeg compound butter log.

PREP TIME: 15 minutes > **TOTAL TIME: 35 minutes** > **YIELD: 12 Servings**

DIRECTIONS

Preheat the oven to 350°F and line a 12-cup muffin tin with cupcake liners. Combine all the dry ingredients, whisk, and set aside. Mix the pumpkin, oil, sour cream, eggs, and honey together in a bowl. Incorporate the dry ingredients with the liquid ingredients. Stir until thoroughly combined. Make the topping by combining the sugar, flour, oats, and cinnamon. Use a fork to cut in the butter and combine the mixture until it resembles breadcrumbs. Put the batter in the cupcake liners three-fourths full, then sprinkle the cinnamon crumble topping onto each muffin. Bake for 20 minutes.

While the muffins are baking, make the compound butter log. Simply combine the softened butter and maple syrup and mix until smooth. Grate the entire nutmeg pod into the softened butter mixture and stir. Let it harden in the fridge for 10 minutes or until workable. Spoon the butter mixture onto an 8-inch piece of waxed paper. Form the butter into a log by folding one side of the paper over the butter and rolling it into a tube, shaping it with your hands on the outside. Place in the refrigerator until firm, then remove the paper and trim off the ends for an even compound butter log. Take the muffins out of the oven and let them cool for 10 minutes, then carefully remove them from the pan and transfer the muffins to a wire cooling rack for 2 minutes. Serve warm with a slice from the delicious nutmeg compound butter log.

INGREDIENTS

2 cups flour

¾ cup brown sugar, packed

1 T. baking powder

1 T. baking soda

2½ tsp. cinnamon

½ tsp. pumpkin pie spice

¼ tsp. salt

1¼ cup pumpkin puree

½ cup vegetable oil

2 T. sour cream

3 eggs

1 T. honey

TOPPING INGREDIENTS

½ cup sugar

½ cup flour

2 T. oats

1 tsp. cinnamon

BUTTER INGREDIENTS

4 T. butter, softened

2 tsp. pure maple syrup

1 whole nutmeg pod

FARM FRESH APPLE FRITTERS

Every fall we load up the entire family and head north for a day trip to the pumpkin patch. We made a tradition of first stopping at the orchard across the lane for their warm apple fritters from the farm stand. They are melt-in-your-mouth delicious, and we have since developed our own fritter recipe so we can enjoy these sweet and tart bites of love anytime we want.

PREP TIME: 25 minutes > TOTAL TIME: 45 minutes > YIELD: 6 Servings

DIRECTIONS

In a medium bowl, whisk together the flour, baking powder, cinnamon, and salt. Set aside.

In a separate bowl, combine the lemon juice and apples. Set aside.

In the bowl of a stand mixer fitted with the paddle attachment, mix the sugar and eggs on medium speed until fully combined. Reduce the speed to low and slowly add the flour mixture and then the milk. Stop the mixer and fold in the apples with a spoon.

Add enough oil to fill a frying pan halfway and heat on medium until the oil reaches 375°F with a candy thermometer. Drop ¼ cup of batter into the oil and let it fry until golden brown. Flip and fry until the opposite side is golden brown. To test for doneness, insert a small knife into the center. If there's still uncooked batter in the center, fry for a bit longer. Transfer to a paper-towel-lined cooling rack and let cool. Repeat with the remaining batter. Make the glaze by combining the sugar, vanilla, and water. Continue to add more water until the mixture is pourable. Drizzle the glaze over the cooled fritters, let dry, and sprinkle powdered sugar on top.

INGREDIENTS

1 cup flour

2 tsp. baking powder

½ tsp. cinnamon

½ tsp. salt

2 tsp. fresh lemon juice

3 Granny Smith apples, peeled, cored, and diced into bite-sized pieces

2 T. granulated sugar

2 large eggs, room temperature

¼ cup whole milk

Vegetable oil for frying

GLAZE INGREDIENTS

1½ cups powdered sugar, sifted, plus 2 T. for sprinkling

½ tsp. vanilla extract

3 tsp. water, or more for preferred consistency

STEAK STEW IN A PUMPKIN

Picking the perfect pumpkin for our steak stew is a family affair. The savory chunks of tender steak and hearty potatoes in this stew are scrumptious. Our kids look forward to this harvest soup because it's cooked and served right out of a pumpkin shell. This is a Sunday supper favorite at our homestead.

PREP TIME: 15 minutes > TOTAL TIME: 4 hours, 15 minutes > YIELD: 8 Servings

DIRECTIONS

Brown the meat in 2 tablespoons oil. In a large pot, add the browned meat, broth, carrots, onion, garlic, bouillon, tomatoes, salt, and pepper. Stir, cover, and simmer for 1 hour. Stir in the potatoes and let simmer another hour.

Meanwhile, wash the pumpkin and cut a circle around the top stem, about 6 to 8 inches in diameter, and remove the top. Remove the fibers and seeds from the top and inside of the pumpkin. We save our seeds for roasting the following day. Place the pumpkin in a shallow, sturdy baking pan. Spoon the stew into the pumpkin and replace the top. Brush the outside of the pumpkin with the final tablespoon of oil. Bake at 325°F for 2 hours or just until the pumpkin is tender. Serve the stew from the pumpkin, scooping out a little pumpkin with each serving.

INGREDIENTS

2 lb. beef stew meat, cut into 1-inch cubes

3 T. oil, divided

1½ cups beef broth

2 cups baby carrots

1½ cups chopped onion

4 tsp. garlic, minced

1 beef bouillon cube dissolved in 1 T. water

1 (14 oz.) can diced tomatoes, undrained

2 tsp. salt

½ tsp. pepper

1 lb. potatoes, peeled and cubed (hack: use 1 [16 oz.] bag frozen cubed hash brown potatoes)

1 pumpkin (approximately 10 pounds)

HAZELNUT FIRESIDE COFFEE

When I was growing up, my mom, my aunt, and their Bible study group would swap friendship teas and coffees. These precious gifts of powdered mixes were given in mason jars, usually with a bow or a sweet message of encouragement attached. It was always a treat for us kids to add heaping spoonfuls of the treasured mix to a mug for a cozy, warm fireside drink. This is a wonderful gift to give or keep for your family. It can also be made with decaf ingredients for kids and late-night fireside chats.

PREP TIME: 10 minutes > **TOTAL TIME: 15 minutes** > **YIELD: 8 Servings**

INGREDIENTS

½ cup dry powdered milk

½ cup powdered hot cocoa mix

¼ cup instant coffee

¾ cup sugar

¼ tsp. cinnamon

½ tsp. finely ground hazelnuts

DIRECTIONS

Mix all ingredients together in a bowl. Blend thoroughly with a whisk and then transfer to a 16 oz. mason jar to give or store.

To enjoy: Mix 3 heaping tablespoons of the coffee mix to 1 cup (8 oz.) hot water. If desired, serve topped with whipped cream and a sprinkle of cinnamon.

S'MORES CRUNCHY CAMPFIRE CONES

If you love sweet and gooey s'mores but are not a fan of the sticky mess, this recipe is for you. Campfire cones have all the melted goodness of s'mores contained in a crunchy sugar cone. Button up your flannel shirt, light the fire, and get ready for some fun! Don't forget your campfire stories.

PREP TIME: 10 minutes > **TOTAL TIME: 15 minutes** > **YIELD: 6 Servings**

DIRECTIONS

Light your campfire outside and place a grate a couple of inches above the flames. In each sugar cone add a layer of marshmallows and then chocolate chips, repeating these layers until the cone is three-fourths full. Wrap each cone with foil and place it on the grate above the fire. Allow it to cook above the flames for about 3 to 5 minutes. Use barbecue tongs to remove the cones from the fire. Be careful when removing the foil because it's hot. Enjoy!

INGREDIENTS

6 sugar ice cream cones

1½ cups mini marshmallows

1 cup chocolate chips

COWBOY BREAKFAST CUPS

A cowboy cup is a simple and hearty breakfast that is fun to make with your family. This cheesy individual ham bowl will keep you full all morning long. You can even allow your family members to customize their cup before it's cooked. Cowboy up!

| PREP TIME: 10 minutes | › | TOTAL TIME: 30 minutes | › | YIELD: 12 Servings |

DIRECTIONS

Preheat the oven to 400°F and grease a 12-cup muffin tin with cooking spray. Line each cup with a slice of ham. In a mixing bowl, add the eggs, cheese, chili powder, half of the chopped green onion, and salt and pepper to taste. Whisk together and pour even amounts into the 12 ham cups. Bake for 15 to 20 minutes.

To serve: Sprinkle a bit of the remaining green onion on each cowboy cup and add a slice of avocado and a spoonful of salsa.

INGREDIENTS

12 pieces of thinly sliced ham

12 large eggs

1 cup shredded cheddar

¼ tsp. chili powder

¼ cup chopped green onion, divided

Salt and pepper to taste

2 avocados, sliced

¼ cup salsa

CAST-IRON CHICKEN POT PIE

Chicken pot pie is a hearty meal and a classic comfort food. Here's a no-fuss recipe with one cast-iron skillet that makes cooking, serving, and cleaning up simple. This rustic dinner can be shared with friends and family on a permanent rotation all season long.

PREP TIME: 20 minutes > TOTAL TIME: 45 minutes > YIELD: 6 Servings

DIRECTIONS

Preheat the oven to 400°F.

Heat the oil in a 10-inch cast-iron skillet (at least 2 inches deep) over medium heat. Add the onion and garlic. Sauté until translucent. Add the hash browns and sauté for 5 minutes. Stir in the peas and carrots. Add the butter and allow it to melt. Sprinkle the flour on top, covering the vegetables, and mix thoroughly. Stir in the cream cheese until it is well-distributed. Pour in the chicken broth and bring everything to a boil. Add the chicken, season with salt and pepper, and remove from heat. Place the pie crust over the chicken and vegetable mixture and carefully press the crust down along the edges of the skillet with your fingers. Don't touch the skillet itself—it will be very hot. Brush the pastry with the egg and cut slits in the top to release steam. Bake for 25 minutes until the top is golden brown.

INGREDIENTS

1 T. olive oil

1 cup white onion, chopped

1 T. minced garlic

1 cup frozen shredded hash browns

1 cup frozen peas

1 cup frozen diced carrots

4 T. butter

4 T. flour

8 oz. cream cheese, softened

2 cups chicken broth

4 cups cooked shredded chicken (I prefer rotisserie chicken with skin included)

Salt and pepper to taste

1 (9-inch) frozen pie crust, thawed

1 egg, beaten

ROSEMARY ROASTED CONCORD CHICKEN

This is one of the easiest and cheapest meals you will find. Yes, you can feed a family of six for under $20! Roasted chicken leg quarters have been a weekly staple at the Grace-Filled Homestead for many years. The herb flavors and warm grapes make this simple dish irresistible to even the pickiest eater.

PREP TIME: 15 minutes > **TOTAL TIME: 4 hours** > **YIELD: 6 Servings**

DIRECTIONS

Preheat the oven to 250°F.

Rub the chicken all over with 1 tablespoon of the olive oil. Season generously with paprika, salt, and pepper. Pour balsamic vinegar into the bottom of the large roasting pan and spread the onion chunks evenly over it. The onions will be used as a flavorful roasting rack. Lay the seasoned chicken on the onions and add 6 rosemary sprigs in between the chicken pieces. Cover the pan with a lid or foil and roast for 3½ hours. Remove from the oven, add the grapes to the pan, and drizzle the grapes with honey. Return to the oven, uncovered, for another 15 to 30 minutes or until the chicken is cooked through and grapes have roasted a bit. Remove from the oven and add the final 6 rosemary sprigs to the dish. Cover the pan and let the chicken rest 5 minutes while the herbs continue to steam and infuse the meal. Serve the chicken with the grapes and even the onion and rosemary if you prefer. Enjoy!

INGREDIENTS

6 chicken leg quarters, skin on

2 T. olive oil, divided

2 tsp. smoked paprika

Salt and pepper to taste

½ cup balsamic vinegar

2 onions, cut into quarters with separated pieces

3 cups seedless grapes (Concord or red preferred)

12 sprigs fresh rosemary, divided

1 T. honey

HEIRLOOM TOMATO TART

We continue to harvest our tomatoes through the fall months, and this dish showcases the flavors of the heirloom varieties. This savory recipe has just the right amount of Gruyère cheese and herbs to complement your fall farm-to-table gathering.

PREP TIME: 20 minutes › **TOTAL TIME: 1 hour, 5 minutes** › **YIELD: 8 Servings**

INGREDIENTS

1 (9-inch) pie crust

2 lb. mixed heirloom tomatoes, sliced ¼ inch thick

1 T. olive oil

3 shallots, thinly sliced

2 tsp. minced garlic

1½ cups shredded Gruyère cheese

¼ cup mayonnaise

1 egg

3 T. breadcrumbs

1 T. chopped fresh chives

1 T. chopped fresh basil

Salt and pepper to taste

DIRECTIONS

Preheat the oven to 375°F.

Coat a 9-inch glass pie dish with cooking spray. Center the pie crust on the dish, folding the overhang and crimping the edges. With a fork, pierce across the bottom of the crust. Choose 6 to 8 tomato slices for the top of the pie. Place them on a baking sheet lined with paper towels. To remove the excess liquid, sprinkle them with salt and press with paper towels on top. Set aside.

Next, roast the tomatoes for the filling in the oven to avoid a soggy pie: Spray a baking rack with cooking spray and place it on a baking sheet. Arrange the filling tomatoes in a single layer on the rack and roast for 45 minutes. While the tomatoes are roasting in the oven, sauté the shallots in the olive oil. When translucent, add the garlic, stir for one minute, and remove from heat.

In a large bowl, thoroughly mix the Gruyère cheese, sautéed shallot mixture, mayo, egg, breadcrumbs, chives, basil, salt, and pepper. Spread half of the Gruyère mixture on the bottom of the pie crust. Gently place the roasted tomatoes evenly atop the cheese layer. Spread the remaining Gruyère mixture over the roasted tomatoes. Finally, arrange the top reserved tomato slices, pressing them down a bit. Bake the heirloom tomato tart for 40 minutes. If needed, use aluminum foil to cover the crust edges. Allow the pie to cool for 1 hour before serving.

SPICED CRÈME PEAR GALETTE

Pear season kicks off the fall harvest at the Grace-Filled Homestead. This rustic pear galette will welcome your guests with autumn scents that are filled with farm-to-table goodness. You can use whatever pear variety is local to your area. This rustic farm dish is loved by foodie friends and grandpa alike.

PREP TIME: 15 minutes › TOTAL TIME: 45 minutes › YIELD: 8 Servings

DIRECTIONS

Preheat the oven to 400°F.

Lightly flour a work surface and roll out the puff pastry sheet into a 10-inch square. Transfer to a baking sheet coated with cooking spray. Fold the corners in and fold over the puff pastry sides, making a round crust for the galette. Remember this foodie dish is better when it's imperfect and rustic, so don't stress on what your folds look like. Bake for 10 minutes.

For the filling, mix the cream cheese, honey, cloves, and ½ teaspoon of the cinnamon in a small bowl. After baking the pastry shell, the pan will be hot, so be careful on this next step: Spread the cream cheese mixture on the inside bottom of the puff pastry. Arrange pear slices over the cream-cheese layer, with slices slightly overlapping each other. Sprinkle sugar and the rest of the cinnamon over the pears and pastry crust. Bake for 20 additional minutes or until golden brown. Serve warm.

INGREDIENTS

1 sheet puff pastry

2 oz. cream cheese, softened

1 T. honey

¼ tsp. ground cloves

1 tsp. ground cinnamon, divided

2 pears, cored and thinly sliced, peel on

1½ T. sugar

AUTUMN APPLE BUTTER

This delicious homemade apple butter is cooked using a slow cooker. It has all the cozy fall flavors that take me back to my childhood. This old-fashioned spread makes a tasty treat slathered on your morning toast or biscuit.

PREP TIME: 30 minutes > TOTAL TIME: 11 hours, 30 minutes > YIELD: 4 (16 oz.) mason jars

DIRECTIONS

Place the apples in a slow cooker. In a medium bowl, mix the sugars, cloves, cinnamon, and salt. Pour the mixture over the apples in the slow cooker and mix well. Cover and cook on high 1 hour. Reduce the heat to low and cook 9 hours, stirring occasionally. Uncover the apple butter, add the vanilla, and stir to the desired consistency. If you desire increased smoothness, use an immersion blender to puree. Continue cooking on low 1 additional hour. Spoon the mixture into jars and tightly seal them. Serve warm immediately or store in the refrigerator for up to a month. Enjoy!

INGREDIENTS

6 pounds of apples, peeled, cored, and chopped finely

1½ cups sugar

1 cup brown sugar

¼ tsp. ground cloves

2 tsp. ground cinnamon

¼ tsp. salt

1 T. vanilla extract

HAM AND CHEESE POPPY SEED SLIDERS

These bite-sized sandwiches are always a hit on game day. The classic ham and cheese flavors are set apart with the delicious poppy seed butter mixture and French fried onions. I know these will be winners in your home just as they are on the Grace-Filled Homestead.

PREP TIME: 10 minutes › TOTAL TIME: 25 minutes › YIELD: 12 sandwiches

DIRECTIONS

Preheat the oven to 350°F. Grease a 9 x 13-inch baking dish. In a bowl, mix the butter, mustard, Worcestershire sauce, poppy seeds, honey, and dried minced onion.

Separate the tops from the bottoms of the rolls and place the bottom pieces into the prepared baking dish. Layer half the ham onto the rolls. Arrange the Swiss cheese over the ham, and top with the remaining ham slices in a layer. Sprinkle the French fried onions evenly over the ham. Place the tops of the rolls onto the sandwiches. Pour the mustard mixture evenly over the top of the rolls. Bake until the rolls are lightly browned and the cheese has melted, about 10 minutes. Slice through the ham and cheese layers into individual rolls to serve.

INGREDIENTS

¾ cup butter, melted

2 T. Dijon mustard

2 tsp. Worcestershire sauce

1½ T. poppy seeds

½ tsp. honey

1 T. dried minced onion

1 cup French fried onions

12 sweet Hawaiian rolls, sliced in half

1 lb. cooked deli ham, thinly sliced

1 lb. Swiss cheese, thinly sliced

GOAT CHEESE FONDUE

Goat cheese is our favorite cheese at the Grace-Filled Homestead, and this recipe is one of the reasons why. This creamy fondue dip is delicious, it's easy to make, and it does not require constant heat like most fondue cheeses.

PREP TIME: 10 minutes › TOTAL TIME: 15 minutes › YIELD: 8 Servings

INGREDIENTS
8 oz. goat cheese
½ cup heavy whipping cream
¼ tsp. salt
1 tsp. honey

DIRECTIONS
In a small pot over low heat, combine the goat cheese and heavy whipping cream. Stir until smooth. Add the honey and salt and stir over low heat for an additional minute. Pour into a fondue pot, dip bowl, or ramekin. Serve with various fruits, veggies, and crackers (our favorites are baguette crackers with pears, grapes, and cucumbers).

RANCH CHILI

This one-dish meal is a hearty treat that even the little ones will love. The ranch dressing flavor keeps your family and friends coming back for more. This is a regular meal at the Grace-Filled Homestead.

PREP TIME: 15 minutes > TOTAL TIME: 1 hour, 5 minutes > YIELD: 12 Servings

DIRECTIONS

In a large pot, brown the ground meat. Add in all the beans and vegetables with all the canning liquids. Mix the ingredients together and simmer over medium heat for 30 minutes. Sprinkle in the taco spice and the ranch dressing mix, stirring as you go. Simmer on low for an additional 20 minutes, stirring regularly. Top with your favorite condiments, such as shredded cheese, sour cream, or hot sauce (if you want more heat in this dish). Serve with cornbread (page 143) or Fritos.

INGREDIENTS

1 lb. ground turkey (or beef if you prefer)

2 cups chopped onion

30 oz. canned red beans

30 oz. canned diced tomatoes

15 oz. canned black beans

15 oz. canned corn

3 T. taco spice

3 T. dried ranch dressing mix (we use Hidden Valley Ranch)

CORNBREAD CAKE WITH WHIPPED HONEY BUTTER

This sweet cornbread can pass for cake any day of the week. The scrumptious honey flavors are infused in the cornbread as well as the whipped butter. Serve warm with your favorite stew, barbecued meat, or chili—or as an afternoon snack on its own.

PREP TIME: 20 minutes > **TOTAL TIME: 55 minutes** > **YIELD: 8 Servings**

DIRECTIONS

Preheat the oven to 350°F. In a mixing bowl, combine the cornmeal, flour, sugar, baking powder, and salt. Add the oil, melted butter, honey, eggs, and milk and whisk well, taking care to fully incorporate the dry ingredients. Pour into a greased baking dish. You can use an 8-inch square pan, muffin tins, a specialty pan, or a round cast-iron skillet. Bake for 35 minutes, or a bit less for muffins. While the cornbread is baking, make the honey butter. Whip the butter, honey, and powdered sugar with a mixer until fluffy. Form into a log or place it in a small dish. Let it firm in the refrigerator for 30 minutes. When the cornbread is done, remove it from the oven and let it sit for 5 minutes. Serve warm with that delicious whipped honey butter on top.

INGREDIENTS

¼ cup cornmeal

1¾ cups flour

1 cup sugar

1 T. baking powder

½ tsp. salt

⅓ cup oil

3 T. butter, melted

1 T. honey

2 eggs, beaten

1¼ cups milk

BUTTER INGREDIENTS

½ lb. (2 sticks) softened butter

¼ cup honey

½ cup powdered sugar

SMOKED ARMADILLO EGGS

Our city is known for barbecue, so we take things up a notch on this version of jalapeño poppers. We cover the cheese-stuffed peppers with sausage and bacon and then throw them on the smoker for a couple of hours. Delicious!

PREP TIME: 25 minutes > TOTAL TIME: 3 hours > YIELD: 6 Servings

INGREDIENTS

6 jalapeños, stem end and seeds removed

4 oz. goat cheese

2 oz. cream cheese, softened

½ cup shredded cheddar cheese

1 lb. pork sausage

12 slices bacon

½ cup your favorite Kansas City BBQ sauce

1 T. Outlaw BBQ rub, separated (page 86)

DIRECTIONS

Preheat the smoker to 275°F. Combine the three cheeses and 1½ teaspoons of the Outlaw BBQ rub seasoning. Fill the jalapeños with the cheese mixture. Use the back of the spoon to press the filling into each jalapeño. In a bowl, combine the pork sausage and 1½ teaspoons of the Outlaw BBQ rub. Wrap each jalapeño with ⅙ of the sausage mixture. Use your hands to ensure the sausage is covering the entire jalapeño. Wrap each sausage-covered jalapeño with 2 pieces of bacon. Because the pepper stem end is cut off, we place the middle of the first piece of bacon over the end of the pepper, covering the opening. This will keep that melted goodness of the cheese mixture from sneaking out during the hot smoking period. We wrap lengthwise, but you can do it however you want. Secure the bacon with a toothpick if needed. Place the bacon-wrapped armadillo eggs on the smoker over indirect heat and close the lid. Smoke until the internal temperature is 160°F, approximately 2½ hours. To get crispier bacon, brush the eggs with your favorite Kansas City barbecue sauce, increase the heat to 375°F, and cook for 10 minutes. Serve with extra barbecue sauce.

SALTED CARAMEL COOKIE CAKE

We all love a good chocolate chip cookie, but this recipe is the best. The sweet, gooey caramel sauce is topped with pink Himalayan salt for a scrumptious melt-in-your-mouth treat. Top this cookie with your favorite vanilla ice cream and add it to the weekly dessert offerings.

PREP TIME: 15 minutes › TOTAL TIME: 30 minutes › YIELD: 12 Servings

DIRECTIONS

Preheat the oven to 375°F and grease a 10-inch cast-iron skillet. You can substitute a greased pizza stone for the skillet by forming a 10-inch circle of dough. In a mixing bowl, cream together the butter, sugars, egg, and vanilla. In a separate bowl, mix the flour, baking soda, salt, and baking powder. Set the mixture aside. Add the flour mixture to the butter mixture and stir until combined. Finally, add the chocolate chips and mix until they are evenly distributed. Press the cookie dough evenly into the cast-iron skillet bottom, forming one large round cookie. Bake for approximately 15 minutes until golden brown. While cooling for 10 minutes, make the salted caramel sauce.

First, in a saucepan, bring the condensed milk and brown sugar to a boil over medium heat, whisking constantly. Reduce the heat to low, whisk in the butter, salt, and vanilla extract, and simmer for 4 minutes. Continue to whisk constantly so it doesn't burn. Remove from the heat.

To serve, top the cookie cake with ice cream scoops and then drizzle caramel sauce over it, sprinkling the top with Himalayan salt.

INGREDIENTS

½ cup salted butter, softened

½ cup sugar

½ cup brown sugar, packed

1 egg

1 tsp. vanilla extract

1½ cups flour

½ tsp. baking soda

¼ tsp. baking powder

½ tsp. salt

1 cup chocolate chips

1½ quarts vanilla ice cream

SAUCE INGREDIENTS

1 (14 oz.) can sweetened condensed milk

1 cup brown sugar

2 T. butter

½ tsp. salt

1 tsp. vanilla extract

1 tsp. large flake pink Himalayan salt

BUTTER PECAN CINNAMON ROLLS

These cinnamon rolls are the best in the land. They are light and fluffy with a rich nutty flavor. The secret melt-in-your-mouth ingredient is butter pecan ice cream. Be advised . . . if you serve these to houseguests, they will stay another night.

PREP TIME: 30 minutes > TOTAL TIME: 2 hours, 20 minutes > YIELD: 12 Servings

DIRECTIONS

Place the ice cream in a small bowl and allow it to sit on the counter to melt.

Pour the warm milk into the bowl of a stand mixer and sprinkle the yeast on top. Add in the sugar, full egg, egg yolk, and melted butter. Mix until well combined. Next, stir in the flour and salt until the dough begins to form. Place the dough hook on the stand mixer and knead the dough on medium speed for 7 minutes. Alternately, you can use your hands to knead the dough for 7 minutes on a well-floured surface. The dough should form into a nice ball and be slightly sticky. Transfer the dough ball to a well-oiled bowl and cover it with plastic wrap. Allow the dough to rise for 1 hour or until doubled in size. During this time, combine the brown sugar and cinnamon into a bowl and set aside.

After the dough has doubled in size, transfer it to a well-floured surface and roll it out into a 12 x 12-inch square. For the filling, first spread the softened butter across the dough, then sprinkle the cinnamon sugar mixture, patting it into the butter and leaving a ¼-inch margin around the edges. Tightly roll up the dough and place it seam side down to seal the edges of the dough. Cut off and discard the ends if needed. Cut into 1-inch sections with a serrated knife or floss. You should get 12 large pieces. Place the cinnamon rolls cut side up in a greased cast-iron skillet. Pour the melted ice cream over the cinnamon rolls, cover them with plastic wrap, and let them rise again for 45 minutes. Preheat the oven to 350°F. Remove the plastic wrap and bake the cinnamon rolls for 20 minutes or until just slightly golden brown on the edges. I underbake them a bit so they stay soft in the middle. Allow them to cool for 10 minutes before frosting. To make the icing, mix all icing ingredients until smooth and spread the mixture over the cinnamon rolls.

INGREDIENTS
¾ cup warm milk

2¼ tsp. quick rise or active yeast

¼ cup sugar

1 egg plus 1 egg yolk, room temperature

¼ cup butter, melted

3 cups flour, plus more for dusting

¾ tsp. salt

½ cup butter pecan ice cream

FILLING INGREDIENTS
4 T. butter, softened

¾ cup brown sugar, packed

2 T. cinnamon

ICING INGREDIENTS
2 cups powdered sugar

4 oz. cream cheese, softened

½ cup butter, softened

2 T. milk

HERB-INFUSED FRIED TURKEY

Each Thanksgiving we gather with up to 40 of our closest friends and family. It's casual chaos at the Grace-Filled Homestead. Of course, everyone brings amazing sides and desserts, but my husband, CJ, is in charge of preparing the star of the show, the turkey. Our lineup includes 1 oven-roasted turkey, 1 smoked turkey, and the all-time favorite herb-infused fried turkey. You know it's a winner when even the teenagers rave about it.

PREP TIME: 30 minutes › TOTAL TIME: 24 hours › YIELD: 12 Servings

BRINE INGREDIENTS

3 lemons

½ cup fresh sage leaves

2 bay leaves

1 T. whole peppercorns

5 large garlic cloves, peeled and smashed

4 quarts water

1 cup kosher salt

1 (10 to 15 lb.) turkey

RUB AND FRYING INGREDIENTS

½ stick of butter

1 T. seasoning salt

1 T. chili powder

1 T. smoked paprika

1 T. garlic salt

2 tsp. ground pepper

Handful each of fresh basil, sage, rosemary and thyme

3 gallons of peanut oil

DIRECTIONS

Prepare the brine ingredients: Add 1 quart (4 cups) of the water to a very large stock pot. Peel the lemons using a vegetable peeler. Place the peels in the pot, saving one peeled lemon for frying. Roughly chop the sage leaves and place them in the pot with the bay leaves, peppercorns, and garlic cloves. Bring the brine to a boil, then stir in the salt until it is dissolved. Reduce the heat and simmer for 5 minutes. Remove the brining liquid from the heat and add the remaining 3 quarts of room-temperature water.

Prepare the turkey for brining: Remove the turkey from its package, remove the giblets from the inside, and pat dry. Once all of the brine mixture is at room temperature, carefully add the turkey to the pot. Make sure the turkey is submerged. If the turkey is floating, weigh it down with a plate or other heavy object. Cover the pot and brine the turkey in the refrigerator for 12 to 24 hours. Remove the turkey from the brine, rinse, and pat dry.

When you're ready to fry your turkey, cut your butter stick into pats. Gently lifting the breast skin, place the pats just under the skin above the breast meat. For the exterior rub, mix the seasoning salt, chili powder, paprika, garlic salt, and pepper together in a small bowl. Use 2 tablespoons of peanut oil to coat the exterior of the turkey with your hands. Now generously sprinkle the rub mixture all over the top, bottom, and sides of the turkey. Massage it in so it coats the entire surface. Add the rest of the peanut oil to your fryer and preheat it to 325°F. Now fill the inside cavity of the bird with one whole peeled lemon and the herbs. Carefully lower the turkey into the fryer with the fryer hook tool. Fry for approximately 5 minutes a pound or until the internal temperature reaches 165°F. Remove the turkey from the oil and let it rest for 15 minutes before carving.

RUSTIC MASHED POTATOES

Creamy mashed potatoes are a classic comfort food and the foundation of many home-cooked meals. We love this version with the skin on. The skins are loaded with nutrients and give this dish some extra texture.

PREP TIME: 10 minutes > **TOTAL TIME: 35 minutes** > **YIELD: 8 Servings**

DIRECTIONS

Wash the potatoes and cut them into 1-inch chunks. Put the potatoes in a medium-sized saucepan and add enough water to cover the potatoes by 2 inches. Place the pan over medium-high heat. Allow the water to come to a boil and then reduce the heat to simmer for 20 minutes or until the potatoes are tender. Strain the potatoes, then return them to the pot or place them in a large bowl. Add the butter, cream cheese, ¼ cup milk, salt, pepper, and chives. Mash using a potato masher or mixer on low speed, adding extra milk a tablespoon at a time until you reach the desired consistency. Serve and enjoy.

INGREDIENTS

6 large russet potatoes

1 stick butter, softened

4 oz. cream cheese, softened

¼ to ½ cup warm milk

2 tsp. salt

½ tsp. pepper

2 tablespoons minced chives

SPICED MULLED APPLE CIDER

We keep a pot of this apple cider warm on our stove throughout the fall months. It's a delicious help-your-self cozy drink that will fill your house with the aromas of fall. Who needs potpourri or a fall candle when you are sipping mulled apple cider?

PREP TIME: 15 minutes > **TOTAL TIME: 1 hour, 5 minutes** > **YIELD: 8 Servings**

DIRECTIONS

Pour the apple cider into a large pot over low heat. Slice the apples and orange and add them to the cider. Add the allspice berries, cinnamon sticks, and the cranberries. Add the sugar and stir it until dissolved. Bring the mixture to a low boil, then reduce the heat to low and simmer for 1 hour. Serve warm immediately or keep warm for hours on the stove or in a crockpot.

INGREDIENTS

1 gallon apple cider

4 apples

1 whole orange

1½ T. allspice berries

5 cinnamon sticks

½ cup fresh cranberries

¾ cup sugar

STUFFED ACORN SQUASH

This fall treat is filled with flavor. The acorn squash makes a perfect bowl for delicious creamy mashed potatoes. Pairing the flavors of cranberries and nutmeg makes this a favorite at the Grace-Filled Homestead.

PREP TIME: 15 minutes > TOTAL TIME: 1 hour, 5 minutes > YIELD: 6 Servings

INGREDIENTS

3 acorn squash

1 T. olive oil

1 tsp. ground nutmeg, divided

6 cups of rustic mashed potatoes
(page 153)

½ cup dried cranberries

2 T. chopped green onions

Salt and pepper to taste

DIRECTIONS

Preheat the oven to 400°F. Line a baking sheet with parchment paper.

Cut the acorn squash in half from stem to point and remove all the seeds. Brush the cavities with olive oil. Season with salt, pepper, and a sprinkle of ground nutmeg, about ½ teaspoon. Turn them flesh side down on the baking sheet and bake for 40 minutes. Remove from the oven and cool slightly before turning upright. Reduce the oven temperature heat to 350°F.

In a large bowl, stir together the mashed potatoes, dried cranberries, and chopped green onion. Fill the acorn squash cavities with the mashed potato mixture. Sprinkle the top with the rest of the nutmeg and salt and pepper to taste, and place back in the oven for an additional 10 minutes. Enjoy!

PUMPKIN PIE WITH SUGARED CRANBERRIES

Homemade pumpkin pie is the traditional fall dessert. This recipe makes a vintage treat extra special with the crust leaves and sugared cranberries. Top with whipped cream for an additional taste of Thanksgiving goodness.

PREP TIME: 20 minutes > TOTAL TIME: 1 hour, 25 minutes > YIELD: 8 Servings

DIRECTIONS

Preheat the oven to 425°F. Lightly flour a surface and roll one pie crust out to an 11-inch circle. Place the dough into a deep, 9-inch pie dish coated in cooking spray. Fold over the edges of the crust and crimp. Poke holes across the bottom of the pie with a fork for ventilation.

In a medium bowl, whisk the pumpkin, sweetened condensed milk, eggs, spices, and salt until smooth. Pour the pumpkin mixture into the crust. Bake 15 minutes, then reduce the oven temperature to 350°F and continue baking 35 to 40 minutes or until a knife inserted an inch from the crust comes out clean. Check periodically and cover the crust with foil if it starts to brown too early. Cool.

Meanwhile, make decorative leaves from the second pie crust: Roll out the second sheet of pie crust dough onto your lightly floured surface. Use cookie cutters or a knife to make your desired top crust leaves. Place them onto a baking sheet lined with parchment paper and bake at 350°F for 10 minutes or until lightly browned. Remove and set aside to cool before topping the pie.

To make the sugared cranberries, first dip them in warmed maple syrup and place them on a piece of parchment paper to for 1 minute. Then roll them in sugar and leave them to dry for 30 minutes. Decorate the pie top with the crust leaves and sugared cranberries.

INGREDIENTS

2 (9-inch) unbaked pie crusts

1 (15 oz.) can pumpkin puree

1 (14 oz.) can sweetened condensed milk

2 eggs

1 tsp. cinnamon

½ tsp. ground ginger

½ tsp. ground nutmeg

½ tsp. salt

TOPPING INGREDIENTS

1 cup fresh cranberries

3 T. maple syrup

Granulated sugar, for rolling

Winter

Winter at the Grace-Filled Homestead is a time to celebrate the birth of our Savior, delight in glorious rest after busy planting and harvest seasons, and plan holiday parties. We have a large family, and during the month of Christmas, we have even larger gatherings with loved ones. When together, we're all about catching up with cousins, pampering Grandma, smooching new babies, and indulging in delicious treats and meals made from scratch.

Anticipation builds as we await the first snowfall to cover our property in a cloak of white. The minute we can bundle up, we head to the huge hill behind the church for an afternoon of sledding and sipping hot cocoa straight from a thermos. Later, cozy blankets warm our bodies, and bowls of hearty soup nourish our souls.

Fresh chestnuts from a local Missouri farm roast over an open fire while we listen to Nat King Cole sing about this very thing. Every sight, sound, and flavor of this season helps us savor our times of reminiscing, hanging vintage decorations, and sharing family traditions. We cherish the peace and joy with those we love.

We've cleaned up the coop, winterized the animal pens, and covered the garden beds with fresh compost. Now we can turn toward the new year and prioritize rest and reflection. As the fruit trees and garden lie dormant, they too are preparing for the season ahead. Welcome, winter, we've waited all year for you!

SUGAR PLUM CREAM CHEESE STUFFED FRENCH TOAST

This decadent recipe is a casserole-style breakfast that's perfect for Christmas morning. The plum jam layered with the cream-cheese mixture is delicious with the French bread and maple syrup. This is a wonderful dish to start off any special occasion or holiday. It can be chilled overnight or baked the same day.

PREP TIME: 15 minutes > TOTAL TIME: 1 hour, 25 minutes > YIELD: 6 Servings

DIRECTIONS

Cut the French bread into 12 (1-inch) slices. Preheat the oven to 350°F. Place the bread slices on a baking sheet and bake for 5 minutes per side or until firm and overly toasted. This will ensure your breakfast isn't soggy. Butter a 13 x 9-inch baking dish.

To make the jam sandwiches, spread cream cheese generously on half of the slices, add the jam, and top with a plain slice of bread.

To prepare the French toast custard, use a mixer to beat the sugar, vanilla, cinnamon, and heavy cream in a large bowl until well blended. Add the eggs, one at a time, mixing well after each addition. Dip the prepared jam sandwiches in the custard, covering both sides, then arrange the coated jam sandwiches in the baking dish. You can cover the pan with plastic wrap and place it in the refrigerator overnight or make immediately.

Bake, uncovered, for 60 minutes or until golden brown. Remove from the oven and sprinkle with powdered sugar. Serve with additional butter and maple syrup.

INGREDIENTS

1 (1 lb.) loaf French bread

8 oz. cream cheese, softened

1 cup plum jam

1¼ cups sugar

2 tsp. cinnamon

1 T. vanilla extract

4 eggs

1 cup heavy cream

Powdered sugar for sprinkling

Maple syrup, to serve

PEPPERMINT BARK

Christmas and candy canes go together. Peppermint bark is a wonderful way to incorporate candy canes into your tray of sweets. It's a delicious traditional treat with chocolate flavors and hints of minty goodness.

PREP TIME: 15 minutes › TOTAL TIME: 1 hour, 20 minutes › YIELD: 12 Servings

DIRECTIONS

Place unwrapped candy canes in a plastic bag. Using a rolling pin, crush the candy canes into small pieces. Set aside. Lay out a sheet of parchment paper on a baking tray.

In a heavy saucepan, melt the regular chocolate over low heat, stirring continuously until smooth. Blend the peppermint extract into the melted chocolate. Pour it onto the parchment paper and spread it evenly with a spatula. Refrigerate for 20 minutes.

In a heavy saucepan, melt the white chocolate over low heat, stirring continuously until smooth. Remove from heat and let it cool for 3 minutes, and then pour it on top of the first chocolate sheet. Spread it evenly with a spatula. Sprinkle the crushed candy on top of the chocolate layers. Slightly push it in so it stays put. Freeze for 45 minutes. Remove the bark from freezer, break it into pieces, and enjoy!

INGREDIENTS

24 mini candy canes

2 cups chocolate chips

¼ tsp. peppermint extract

2 cups white chocolate chips

ROASTED CHESTNUTS

This is one of our favorite holiday traditions. If you are wondering what all the buzz is about in the vintage Christmas songs and Hallmark movies, it's time to find out. Chestnuts are harvested in the fall and should be refrigerated until you are ready to roast them. We purchase our chestnuts from a local farm in Missouri, but you can find them on local farms across the country.

PREP TIME: 15 minutes > TOTAL TIME: 25 minutes > YIELD: 12 Servings

DIRECTIONS

Rinse the chestnuts to clean and soften the shell. Next, toss the nuts into a bowl of water. This process helps determine if you have any undesirable nuts. Good chestnuts will usually sink, and rotten or moldy ones will float. Discard any that are floating or cracked. Once they are clean, place the nuts on a cutting board, flat side down. With a sharp knife, score each chestnut with an X on the round side. This allows steam to escape when cooking.

Next, put the nuts in a chestnut pan or cast-iron skillet, flat side down. Prepare your open fire so there is a bed of coals or a grate to cook on. The chestnuts and pan heat up quickly, so be prepared in advance with your potholders. Cook the chestnuts for five minutes and then use tongs to turn each chestnut over and cook for another five minutes. Chestnuts are easiest to peel when they are warm. As soon as you can handle them, peel off the shell and the papery covering underneath.

Although most people love to eat the chestnuts after they are peeled right off the fire, others like to chop and add them to their favorite recipes. Chestnuts have a rustic flavor and bring an earthy taste to pesto, soups, and roasted meats.

INGREDIENTS
2 lb. chestnuts

BAKED BRIE WITH CRANBERRY PUFF PASTRY

The family begs for this elegant yet rustic appetizer at every holiday event. It is a family staple and is usually gone within 2 minutes. The melted cheese mixes with the fruit in a delicious flaky crust. It is pure heaven to your tastebuds.

PREP TIME: 10 minutes > **TOTAL TIME: 35 minutes** > **YIELD: 8 Servings**

INGREDIENTS

8 oz. Brie cheese round
(about 4 inches in diameter)

1 sheet frozen puff pastry, thawed

⅓ cup whole berry cranberry sauce

1 egg, lightly whisked for
an egg wash

DIRECTIONS

Preheat the oven to 425°F. Remove the rind off the top of the Brie round with a sharp knife. Place the puff pastry sheet on a piece of parchment paper. Use a rolling pin to roll out the seams and make it as square as possible. Spread a 4-inch circle of cranberry sauce in the center of the puff pastry. Place the Brie cut side down right on top of the cranberry sauce. Fold the sides of the pastry circle up to meet in the center, going around in one direction, until the Brie is completely covered. Press the seams together. This is rustic, so don't worry if the seams don't come together perfectly. Flip the pastry cheese round over so the smooth side is facing up, and place it, along with the parchment paper, in the center of a baking sheet.

With a pastry brush, apply the egg wash to the top and sides of the puff pastry. Bake for 25 minutes or until golden brown. Serve with your favorite crackers or crostini.

BUTTERMILK BISCUITS AND SAGE SAUSAGE GRAVY

Christmas morning at the Grace-Filled Homestead always includes our traditional Bs & Gs. After the gifts are opened and the floor is covered in crinkled wrapping paper, we head into the kitchen for a delicious breakfast spread. The flaky buttermilk biscuits are warm just out of the oven, but the real showstopper is the sage sausage gravy.

PREP TIME: 30 minutes > TOTAL TIME: 45 minutes > YIELD: 12 Servings

DIRECTIONS FOR BISCUITS

Place 2 full sticks of butter in the freezer for 20 minutes before starting, then cut it into ½-inch cubes. This ensures light and flaky biscuits. Preheat the oven to 400°F and line a baking sheet with parchment paper.

In a large bowl, combine the flour, baking powder, and salt. Use a pastry cutter or a fork to incorporate the frozen butter into the flour mixture, leaving big chunks. Add the buttermilk and stir until combined without overworking the dough. Add a tiny splash of extra buttermilk if the dough is too dry.

Flour your countertop and roll the dough to a 1½-inch thickness. Using a 2-inch biscuit cutter or mason jar rim, cut the dough into rounds. Place the biscuits on the baking sheet so they are touching. Combine and reroll any scraps to form additional biscuits. Bake for 15 minutes. Melt the remaining 2 tablespoons of butter and brush it on the hot biscuits immediately after removing them from the oven.

DIRECTIONS FOR GRAVY

Brown the sausage in a large skillet over medium heat until cooked thoroughly. Sprinkle the sage and flour evenly over the sausage and stir over medium heat for 2 minutes. Pour in the milk a cup at a time, stirring frequently until reaching your desired thickness, up to 15 minutes. Add salt and pepper to taste. Spoon the gravy over halved warm biscuits and serve with fruit.

INGREDIENTS

1 cup (2 sticks) plus 2 T. unsalted butter, divided

4 cups all-purpose flour, plus more for work surface

3 T. baking powder

1 tsp. salt

1½ cups cold buttermilk

GRAVY INGREDIENTS

1 lb. breakfast sausage

2 T. dried sage

⅓ cup flour

4 cups whole milk

Salt and pepper to taste

MEEMA'S CHICKEN NOODLE SOUP

This family recipe is a special part of our Christmas tradition. Once the extended family has celebrated separately during the day, we all head to Grandma's house on Christmas night to hug on new babies, see the cousins, and enjoy a bowl of steaming joy. It's a simple one-pot wonder that tastes delicious and brings a huge family together on a special holiday.

PREP TIME: 15 minutes > TOTAL TIME: 50 minutes > YIELD: 18 Servings

DIRECTIONS

Melt the butter in a large pot over medium heat. Sauté the onions, celery, carrots, and garlic in the butter until the veggies soften and the onions become translucent, approximately 10 minutes. Stir in the thyme, salt, and pepper. Add the flour and cook, stirring, for 2 minutes. Whisk in the chicken broth and bay leaves and bring to a simmer. Add the frozen egg noodles, heavy cream, and cooked chicken. Cook over low heat for 25 minutes or until the noodles are cooked through. Remove the bay leaves and serve with rolls.

INGREDIENTS

8 T. butter

2 onions, chopped

4 cups celery, chopped

4 cups carrots, peeled and chopped

3 garlic cloves, chopped

1 tsp. dried thyme

2 tsp. kosher salt

1 tsp. pepper

4 T. flour

12 cups chicken broth

2 bay leaves

24 oz. frozen egg noodles

2 cups of heavy cream

6 cups cooked chicken, diced or chopped (we use rotisserie chicken and include the skin)

SKILLET NO-KNEAD DINNER ROLLS

There is nothing better than a soft and fluffy dinner roll right out of the warm oven. These simple no-knead rolls are scrumptious with a buttery flavor. They are a wonderful winter addition to serve with soups or stews, and they even make great sandwiches.

PREP TIME: 20 minutes > **COOK TIME: 2 hours, 40 minutes** > **YIELD: 16 Servings**

DIRECTIONS

In a small saucepan, warm the milk and sugar over medium heat until the sugar is dissolved. Add in the oil and remove from heat. When the milk mixture is cooled to a lukewarm temperature (100°F), transfer it to a mixing bowl and use a wooden spoon to add the yeast and flour one cup at a time until fully combined. Use lightly floured hands to fold the edges of the dough in toward the middle until a smooth ball is formed. Flip the dough ball over seam side down. Cover the bowl and allow it to rest at room temperature for 1 hour or until the dough doubles in size. Add the salt, baking powder, and baking soda to the dough. Mix until combined.

Place the dough onto a floured surface and divide it into 16 pieces. Shape each piece into a ball by gathering up the sides, and again folding the edges toward the middle until a smooth ball is formed. Arrange them in a lightly oiled 10- or 12-inch cast-iron skillet, sides touching. Cover the dish with a tea towel and let the dough rise for 1 hour.

Preheat your oven to 400°F. If you like the top of your rolls browned, brush each dough ball with the whisked egg. Bake for 18 minutes or until they are golden brown on top. Brush the tops of the rolls with melted butter and serve.

INGREDIENTS

1½ cups milk

2 T. sugar

3 oz. vegetable oil

1 (¼ oz.) package of active dry yeast

3 cups bread flour, plus about 2 T. for surface

2 tsp. kosher flake salt

½ tsp. baking powder

½ tsp. baking soda

1 egg for egg wash, optional

1 T. melted butter

HOLIDAY CRANBERRY TEA

This beverage is a regular feature at our Christmas and New Year's festivities. It is extremely simple to make and absolutely delicious. These instructions are for a pitcher, but you can also double the recipe for a larger drink dispenser or punch bowl.

PREP TIME: 5 minutes › TOTAL TIME: 5 minutes › YIELD: 8 Servings

DIRECTIONS

Pour the iced tea and Sprite into a glass pitcher. Stir to combine. Add one cup of ice and then the fresh cranberries. Stir again to combine. Finally, add the cranberry juice and the last cup of ice to the top. Pour into chilled glasses and add three cranberries to each glass for a garnish. Enjoy this delicious drink.

INGREDIENTS

1 cup iced tea

9 cups Sprite or your favorite lemon lime soda

¼ cup cranberry juice

1 cup fresh cranberries, plus extra for garnish

2 cups ice

ICED GINGERBREAD FOREST CAKE

This rustic cake marries vintage cool-weather spices with a cream cheese frosting, sugared cranberries, and a forest of rosemary. Enjoy a piece of this gingerbread cake as you cozy up to the fireplace.

PREP TIME: 30 minutes > TOTAL TIME: 1 hour, 30 minutes > YIELD: 8 Servings

DIRECTIONS FOR CAKE

Preheat the oven to 350°F. Butter and flour three 6-inch baking pans.

In a large bowl, whisk together the flour, baking powder, sugar, cinnamon, ginger, cloves, nutmeg, baking soda, and salt.

In a medium bowl, whisk the eggs until lightly beaten. Add the honey and molasses and whisk until combined, then whisk in the milk, water, and melted butter.

Add the wet mixture to the dry mixture, mix just until combined. Divide the batter evenly between the cake pans and bake for about 25 to 30 minutes. Let the cakes cool for 15 minutes and then unmold them onto a cooling rack. Refrigerate for 20 minutes.

DIRECTIONS FOR TOPPING

Warm the maple syrup in a small bowl. Lay out a piece of parchment paper and place a shallow layer of sugar on a plate. Dip the berries and rosemary sprigs in maple syrup and place them on the parchment paper for 1 minute. Roll them in sugar and leave them to dry for 30 minutes.

DIRECTIONS FOR FROSTING

Beat the cream cheese and butter for 1 minute. Slowly add the powdered sugar and vanilla, and whip the frosting until fluffy.

CAKE ASSEMBLY

Remove rounded cake layer tops with a serrated knife. Put the first cake layer on a cake stand or plate and spread a thick layer of frosting on it using an offset spatula. Keep doing this until you've frosted all three cake layers, including the top of the last layer. Spread a thin layer of frosting around the sides of the cake and put it in the fridge to set for 10 minutes. Top the cake with sugared cranberries and rosemary.

INGREDIENTS

2⅓ cups all-purpose flour

1½ tsp. baking powder

¾ cup sugar

1 tsp. ground cinnamon

1 tsp. ground ginger

½ tsp. ground cloves

½ tsp. ground nutmeg

½ tsp. baking soda

Pinch of salt

2 large eggs

⅓ cup honey

⅓ cup molasses

½ cup milk

½ cup water

8 T. (1 stick) unsalted butter, melted

TOPPING INGREDIENTS

1 cup fresh cranberries

10 sprigs rosemary

3 T. maple syrup

Granulated sugar, for rolling

FROSTING INGREDIENTS

8 oz. cream cheese, softened

6 T. butter, softened

4 cups powdered sugar

2 tsp. vanilla extract

STRAWBERRY JALAPEÑO JAM OVER GOAT CHEESE

Here at the homestead, we love all things goat cheese, but this starter earns GOAT status. You'll be the hit of the next holiday party when you show up with this one, and I promise you will be leaving with an empty plate. You can tweak the heat level to be as spicy as you like.

TOTAL TIME: 25 minutes › **YIELD: 8 Servings**

DIRECTIONS

Wash canning jars and lids in hot soapy water, rinse well, and dry.

Place the strawberries, jalapeños, lemon juice, and pectin into a large saucepan and bring to a full boil over high heat. Once boiling, stir in the sugar until it is dissolved, return the jam to a full boil, and cook for 1 minute. Use a ladle to pour the hot jam into jars and cover tightly with lids. Allow the jam to sit at room temperature for 24 hours to set, then refrigerate for up to a month.

When it's time to share, place your chilled log of goat cheese on a serving dish. Pour strawberry jalapeño jam over the goat cheese. If you would like to add more spice to this starter, sprinkle a few drops of your favorite hot sauce on top of the jam. Serve with your favorite crackers or crostini.

INGREDIENTS

4 cups strawberries, hulled and crushed

1 cup minced jalapeño peppers

¼ cup lemon juice

1.75 oz. powdered fruit pectin

7 cups white sugar

4 (16 oz.) canning jars with lids

8 oz. goat cheese log

Hot sauce to taste

HERB-ENCRUSTED PRIME RIB WITH ROSEMARY HORSERADISH SAUCE

Prime rib is for special occasions. Many reserve this treat for a holiday, but for us, it's a delicious splurge for a birthday dinner. Two of our sons share a birthday week in January. Herb-encrusted prime rib is the foundation to a wonderful celebration. The creamy rosemary horseradish sauce is a tangy addition that takes this meal to the next level.

TOTAL TIME: 4 hours, 30 minutes > YIELD: 10 servings

DIRECTIONS

Let the meat rest at room temperature for 2 hours. Preheat the oven to 500°F. Remove the silver skin membrane where possible. Place a roasting rack on a baking sheet to catch the juices while the meat cooks. Prepare the wet rub by mixing together the mustard, olive oil, salt, pepper, garlic, rosemary, and thyme. Coat the roast with the wet rub. Place the prime rib roast on the roasting rack and cook for 5 minutes per pound (30 minutes for a 6-pound roast). Turn the oven off and do not open the door. Let the roast sit in warm oven for 2 hours.

About a half hour before you plan to eat, prepare the sauce: Mix the sour cream, horseradish, mayonnaise, rosemary, salt, and pepper in a bowl. Refrigerate for 20 minutes before serving. Remove the prime rib from the oven. If using a meat thermometer, 115 to 125°F is rare and 130 to 140°F is medium. Slice the steaks one inch thick. Serve with sauce on the side.

MEAT AND RUB INGREDIENTS

6 lb. prime rib roast

5 oz. stone-ground mustard

3 T. olive oil

⅓ cup salt

2 T. pepper

2 T. minced garlic

2 T. chopped rosemary

2 T. chopped thyme

SAUCE INGREDIENTS

½ cup sour cream

3 T. prepared horseradish

2 T. chopped rosemary

2 T. mayonnaise

Salt and pepper to taste

POMEGRANATE BRUSSELS SPROUTS

As a child I despised brussels sprouts, but now they are a family favorite. When they are prepared with fresh pomegranates and local honey, the sweetness permeates every bite. And who could resist the rich bacon crumbles? If you've ever doubted the lure of brussels sprouts, this recipe is one to try.

PREP TIME: 10 minutes > TOTAL TIME: 40 minutes > YIELD: 6 Servings

DIRECTIONS

Preheat the oven to 400˚F. Trim the ends of the brussels sprouts and cut them in half lengthwise. Whisk the olive oil, garlic, honey, whipping cream, and pomegranate juice in a medium to large bowl. Add the brussels sprouts into the dressing and toss to coat. Lay them on a baking sheet or roasting pan, and sprinkle with salt and pepper.

Roast the sprouts for 20 minutes, toss them with the crumbled bacon, and return them to the oven for another 5 to 10 minutes or until they start browning. Garnish with pomegranate seeds and serve warm.

INGREDIENTS

1½ lb. brussels sprouts

3 T. olive oil

3 tsp. minced garlic

3 T. honey

¼ cup heavy whipping cream

1 T. pomegranate juice

Salt and pepper to taste

8 pieces cooked bacon, chopped

¼ cup pomegranate seeds

STOVETOP HOT COCOA

Hot cocoa is a winter tradition. We developed this recipe out of necessity one year when the kiddos were little. There was an unexpected ice storm and most of our hometown lost electricity for two days. We hunkered down around the fireplace, warm and toasty, playing games by candlelight. Although most appliances did not work, we still had use of our gas stove for hot cocoa. We had so much fun during that storm, we were a bit bummed when the electricity came back on.

TOTAL TIME: 5 minutes > YIELD: 8 Servings

INGREDIENTS

1 cup sugar

½ cup unsweetened cocoa powder

8 cups whole milk, divided

1 tsp. vanilla extract

2 cups whipped cream

½ tsp. cinnamon

4 candy canes, crushed

DIRECTIONS

Whisk the sugar, cocoa, and 1 cup of milk in a pot. Bring to a boil over medium heat and stir for 2 minutes. Add the remaining milk and stir until hot. Turn off the heat and whisk in the vanilla. Fill mugs with hot cocoa. Top with whipped cream, cinnamon, and crushed candy canes.

PESTO CHICKEN WITH SUN-DRIED TOMATOES

This garlic-marinated chicken layered with spinach, fresh basil pesto, and sun-dried tomatoes is a delicious treat to indulge your sweetie. When cutting into that flaky puff pastry, there is just the right amount of melted cheese to melt your heart. This has been one of the kiddos' favorite dishes for years.

PREP TIME: 20 minutes › TOTAL TIME: 4 hours, 30 minutes › YIELD: 8 servings

DIRECTIONS

Combine the garlic and the egg yolks in a small bowl. Cut each chicken breast in half with the butterfly method making 8 equal portions. To butterfly a breast into two pieces, lay it flat on a cutting board, place one hand on the top and with a sharp knife cut horizontally all the way through leaving you with the original shape of the breast but half as thick. Place the chicken breasts in a shallow glass dish and cover both sides with the egg and garlic mixture. Cover the dish with plastic wrap and refrigerate 3½ hours.

When the chicken has fully marinated, preheat the oven to 375°F. Grease a baking sheet.

Place one half-sheet of puff pastry on a lightly floured board. Place ½ cup of spinach in the center of the pastry sheet. Remove one piece of chicken breast from the marinade, shaking off any excess, and place it on top of the spinach. Spread 1 tablespoon of pesto over the chicken, layer with ⅛ cup of sun-dried tomatoes, and sprinkle ⅛ cup of feta cheese on top. Fold the pastry around the chicken and use your fingers or a fork to seal the pastry seam. Place the bundle seam side down on the baking sheet. Repeat these steps with the other half-sheets of puff pastry to make 8 identical bundles of chicken. Bake for 40 minutes and serve warm.

INGREDIENTS

5 T. minced garlic

2 egg yolks

4 boneless skinless chicken breast

4 frozen puff pastry sheets, thawed, cut in half

4 cups chopped fresh spinach

½ cup prepared basil pesto (page 64)

1 cup chopped sun-dried tomatoes

1 cup crumbled feta cheese

HOT BACON VINAIGRETTE SPINACH SALAD

My introduction to a warm bacon vinaigrette was during my college waitressing days at a local diner. Spinach leaves drenched in hot herb and bacon vinaigrette is a scrumptious starter. Who knew a salad could taste so delicious? For years after I graduated and left my serving days behind, I was on the pursuit to recreate this dish. This salad can be served before dinner, or it can command center stage as the main course.

PREP TIME: 5 minutes › TOTAL TIME: 25 minutes › YIELD: 4 Servings

DIRECTIONS

In a large skillet, cook the bacon over medium heat until browned and crisp. Do not drain the grease. Break up the bacon into inch-sized crumbles in the pan and add the olive oil to the warm pan. Remove the skillet from the heat and stir in the mustard, onions, vinegar, and thyme. Pour the chunky, warm dressing into a large bowl. Add the spinach, season with salt and pepper, and toss the spinach with the dressing to evenly coat the leaves. Add the nuts and cheese and lightly toss again. Transfer the salad to plates and serve.

INGREDIENTS

8 strips thickly sliced bacon

2 T. olive oil

2 T. stone ground mustard

¼ cup minced onion

3 T. red wine vinegar

1 T. fresh thyme, or 1 tsp. dried

8 cups baby spinach

Salt and pepper to taste

½ cup roasted pecans, coarsely chopped

4 oz. crumbled blue cheese

RANCH BREAKFAST BASKETS

Whether you are herding cattle on a ranch or rushing your way to the office, this protein-packed breakfast will give you the energy to git 'er done. These cheesy potato baskets are filled with bacon, an egg, and lots of flavor and can be made in advance for a quick and easy morning.

PREP TIME: 15 minutes > TOTAL TIME: 1 hour, 25 minutes > YIELD: 6 Servings

DIRECTIONS

Preheat the oven to 400°F. Wash the potatoes and use a fork to pierce them in several places to allow steam to escape as they bake. Place the potatoes directly on the oven rack and bake for 40 minutes or until tender. Cool for about 10 minutes. Slice each potato in half lengthwise and hollow out each half, scooping the potato flesh into a mixing bowl. Save the skins to serve as your baskets. Add the butter and cream to the potato flesh and mash together until smooth. Season with salt and pepper.

Spread 1 tablespoon of the potato mixture into the bottom of each hollowed potato skin basket and sprinkle with 1 tablespoon of cheese. Be sure to leave room for the bacon and egg. You may have some left-over potato mixture that you can save or discard. Add a slice of bacon to each basket and lightly push down the filling with a spoon to make room to top the bacon with a raw egg, keeping the yolks and whites intact. Place the loaded potatoes onto a baking sheet. Lower the oven temperature to 375°F and bake the potatoes until the egg whites are just set and the yolks are still runny, approximately 20 minutes. Top each potato with a sprinkle of the remaining cheese and finish with green onions, salt, and pepper. Serve with sour cream and hot sauce of your choice.

INGREDIENTS

3 medium russet potatoes

3 T. butter, softened

3 T. heavy cream

1/2 cup shredded cheddar

6 slices thick-cut bacon, cooked

6 medium eggs

¼ cup chopped green onion

Salt and pepper to taste

Sour cream and hot sauce, to serve

CREAMY BAKED POTATO SOUP

This soup is the ultimate loaded baked potato soup. Our kiddos regularly ask for this meal, even from the dorm room or fire station. This hearty soup is topped with cheese, green onions, and bacon chunks. Can you imagine anything better? Serve with your favorite crusty bread or dinner rolls.

PREP TIME: 15 minutes > TOTAL TIME: 35 minutes > YIELD: 12 Servings

DIRECTIONS

Melt both sticks of butter in a saucepan. Add the celery and onion and sauté for 2 minutes over medium heat. Transfer the mixture to a large stock pot and add the half-and-half and heavy whipping cream. Add the garlic, salt, and pepper. Bring to a boil and then add the cubed potatoes and ham. Reduce the heat to low and stir continuously for 20 minutes or to desired consistency. Serve topped with cheddar cheese, bacon crumbles, and sliced green onions.

INGREDIENTS

2 sticks butter

3 stalks celery, chopped

1 onion, chopped

8 cups half-and-half

1 cup heavy whipping cream

1 T. minced garlic

2 tsp. salt

1 tsp. pepper

4 cups peeled and cubed potatoes
(hack:1 large bag of cubed
frozen hash brown potatoes)

4 cups cubed ham

3 cups cheddar cheese, shredded

3 lb. bacon, cooked and crumbled

6 green onions, chopped

CHERRY CRÈME STRUDEL

A cream cheese breakfast strudel has always been one of my husband's favorite morning indulgences. This rustic sweet pastry is light and creamy with just the right amount of tart cherry filling and nutty goodness.

PREP TIME: 15 minutes > **TOTAL TIME: 1 hour, 25 minutes** > **YIELD: 8 Servings**

INGREDIENTS

4 oz. cream cheese, softened

3 T. sugar

½ tsp. almond extract

¼ cup sliced almonds

1 (8 oz.) can refrigerated crescent rolls

1 cup cherry pie filling

1 cup powdered sugar

3 tsp. milk

DIRECTIONS

Preheat the oven to 375°F and coat a cookie sheet with nonstick cooking spray.

Beat the cream cheese and granulated sugar until light and fluffy. Stir in the almond extract and set aside.

Unroll the crescent dough package onto a cookie sheet; press into a 13 x 7-inch rectangle, firmly pressing the perforations to seal smooth. Spoon the cream cheese mixture lengthwise down the center third of the dough rectangle. Then layer the cherry pie filling over the cream cheese mixture. On each long side of the dough rectangle, make cuts 1 inch apart to the edge of the filling. Fold opposite strips of dough over the filling and cross them in the center to form a braided appearance. Seal the ends by firmly pressing the dough together.

Bake the strudel 20 minutes or until golden brown. Move it from the cookie sheet to a cooling rack. Cool completely, about 30 minutes. In small bowl, mix the powdered sugar and milk to make an icing, and drizzle it over the strudel. Garnish with sliced almonds, slice, and serve warm with a hot cup of coffee.

RUSTIC FROMAGE FLATBREAD

This fromage flatbread allows you to blend your favorite flavors for an easy-to-make rustic meal. Mozzarella is the delicious cheese foundation, but we always layer in another favorite cheese as well. We don't always add sauce, but you could add a red or alfredo sauce. Because this recipe makes 6 individual flatbreads, it's fun to make a flatbread topping bar so your friends and family can customize their toppings.

PREP TIME: 50 minutes > TOTAL TIME: 1 hour, 5 minutes > YIELD: 6 Servings

DIRECTIONS

Preheat the oven to 475°F. In the bowl of a stand mixer, combine the flour, garlic powder, yeast and salt. Then add 2 tablespoons of the olive oil and the water. Beat with the paddle attachment on low speed for 4 minutes as it all combines roughly into a dough ball. Transfer the dough to a lightly floured work surface and knead with lightly floured hands for 1 minute. Depending on the humidity in your area, you may need to add 1 more tablespoon of flour if the dough is too sticky to handle or add 1 tablespoon of water if the dough is too dry.

Divide the dough into 6 equal pieces. On a lightly floured surface, use floured hands to begin shaping and stretching one piece of dough at a time until it is less than ¼ inch thick. The thinner the better for flat bread. You can use a floured rolling pin for this too. Don't worry about the shape of the dough; just make sure it's thin. These will be 6 individual rustic flatbreads. Dust 2 large baking sheets with cornmeal and place 3 individual flatbread crusts on each sheet.

Using a fork, prick a few holes in the flat dough. Precook your dough for 5 minutes. Brush each with a small amount of olive oil. Top each flatbread with 3 slices of mozzarella. Then add your customized toppings. Bake for 10 to 15 minutes or until the crust and toppings are browned to your liking. Remove from the oven. Slice and serve warm.

INGREDIENTS

3 cups all-purpose flour, plus more for kneading

1 tsp. garlic powder

.25 oz. (2¼ tsp. or 1 packet) instant yeast

1¼ tsp. salt

3 T. olive oil, divided

1 cup warm water

Cornmeal for dusting

16 oz. log of mozzarella, sliced

Your favorite toppings

OUR FAMILY'S FAVORITE FLAVORS

Tomato, pesto, basil, Parmesan flakes

Arugula, goat cheese, balsamic reduction, walnuts

Spinach, gorgonzola, artichoke hearts, caramelized red onions

CHARCUTERIE BOARD WITH PEPPERONI ROSES

A charcuterie board has become a favorite way to serve up snacks. It allows guests to graze and enjoy little bites of their various favorites. Of course, a pepperoni rose tastes much better than just a few slices of meat on a board. We serve this board all through the holidays and again in late winter. Roses are always a hit around Valentine's Day. Who wouldn't want a dozen pepperoni roses?

PREP TIME: 25 minutes › **YIELD: 8 Servings**

DIRECTIONS

To make the pepperoni roses, first set a glass in front of you and start folding individual slices of pepperoni over the rim of the glass. A small-mouthed glass works best. I use a champagne flute. Half the slice should be on the inside of the rim and half outside. Overlap the slices, covering about half the first slice with the next slice and continuing around, holding them down tightly so they hug the rim. You will need about 10 to 12 slices for each rose, making several layers of pepperoni. Once the pepperoni is in multiple layers all the way around the rim of the glass, place a paper towel over the top, fold down the outside, and secure it with a rubber band. Repeat the process with additional glasses and pepperoni slices for as many roses as you'd like to make. Place the glasses in the refrigerator to set for about 15 minutes. Once chilled, remove the rubber band and paper towel. Turn the glass upside down and set it down, carefully removing the pepperoni rose from the glass.

On the charcuterie tray, arrange your pepperoni roses with the cheese and crackers, and then add olives, nuts, and other favorite finger foods. Add small containers filled with your favorite honey and mustard. Don't forget to add utensils for cutting and serving your delicious treats.

INGREDIENTS

7 oz. pepperoni slices or thin salami slices

Various sliced cheeses

Various block cheeses

2 different types of your favorite crackers

25 kalamata olives

25 green olives

½ cup mixed nuts

½ cup berries, pickles, or artichoke hearts

4 oz. honey

4 oz. stone ground mustard

CHOCOLATE-COVERED STRAWBERRIES

Strawberries are one of our favorite treats at the Grace-Filled Homestead. I have fond childhood memories of picking berries with my mom in her strawberry patch. The combination of sweet berries and rich chocolate can't be beat. We like ours plain and simple, but you could add sprinkles or drizzle white chocolate before they set firm. During the season of love, pamper your sweetie with this simple and delicious treat.

PREP TIME: 15 minutes > TOTAL TIME: 45 minutes > YIELD: 8 Servings

DIRECTIONS

Begin by rinsing your strawberries. Allow them to dry fully on a paper towel. Line a baking sheet with parchment paper. Melt your chocolate a few pieces at a time on low heat, stirring constantly, approximately 5 minutes, until smooth. When the chocolate is completely melted, remove it from the heat. Place the strawberries right next to your pan.

Hold your pot of chocolate at an angle. Grab a strawberry by the stem, dip both sides in the chocolate, and place it on your parchment paper. Repeat with all the strawberries, leaving the top of the berry and stem uncoated. Let the strawberries sit on the counter for 30 minutes. Enjoy!

INGREDIENTS
1 pint strawberries

8 oz. melting chocolate
(pure or almond bark)

BROWNIE TRIFLE BOWL

This chocolate dessert is almost too pretty to eat . . . almost! Your loved ones will know how special they are when they see the rich layers of decadent brownies, whipped cream, and chocolate pudding. The chocolate shavings and pomegranate topping spread joy and love with every bite.

PREP TIME: 15 minutes › TOTAL TIME: 45 minutes › YIELD: 12 Servings

INGREDIENTS

1 cup butter, melted

2 cups granulated sugar

½ cup cocoa powder

1 tsp. vanilla extract

4 eggs

1½ cups all-purpose flour

½ tsp. baking powder

½ tsp. salt

4 cups cold milk

2 (3.9 oz.) packages instant chocolate pudding mix

5 cups whipped cream

Chocolate shavings and pomegranate seeds to garnish

DIRECTIONS FOR BROWNIES

Preheat the oven to 350°F. To start the brownies, grease a 9 x 13-inch pan. Combine the melted butter, sugar, cocoa powder, vanilla, eggs, flour, baking powder, and salt. Spread the batter evenly in the pan. Bake the brownies for 25 minutes or until a toothpick inserted in the center comes out clean. Cool.

DIRECTIONS FOR PUDDING

Pour the cold milk into a large bowl. Add the pudding mix and beat for 5 minutes or until set. Refrigerate the pudding until you are ready to assemble the trifle.

TRIFLE ASSEMBLY

Cut the cooled brownies into small squares. In a large dessert bowl (a glass bowl will let you see the delicious layers), layer half the brownies, half the whipped cream, and all the chocolate pudding. Repeat with another layer of brownies, then a top layer of whipped cream. Top the whipped cream with some chocolate shavings and pomegranate seeds. Serve immediately or store in the fridge until ready to serve.

Apothecary Pantry

The apothecary pantry at the Grace-Filled Homestead is often referred to as our Farmacy. It's filled with foraged teas, preserved vegetables, fruit jams, dried herbs, fermented treats, and scratch concoctions for whatever ails you. There is nothing better than a gently bubbling jar of fruit kombucha, elderberry syrup, or fire cider to help with the first signs of a cold. Drying herbs and tending your sourdough starter are traditions that create more self-sufficiency and peace in your home.

If you're looking for a sustainable, low-tech method of preserving food, I'll introduce you to a couple of easy fermentation recipes. These preservation methods have been passed down through different societies for generations. There are so many economic and health benefits to having your own Farmacy, whether you live on a 100-acre ranch or in a downtown apartment. You can start small. It will only take up a small corner of your kitchen, improve your health, and save you time and money. Let's get back to the basics of the apothecary pantry.

DRIED HERBS

Enjoy the flavors of summer all year long with dried herbs. The peak time to cut herbs is right before flowering, when the aromatic and flavorful oil content is at its highest. We prefer to hang our herbs to dry. There are many other methods to dry your herbs, such as dehydrators or oven use. The ancient method of hanging your herbs to dry is simple, and it allows us to enjoy the beauty and aromas a few extra weeks each season.

PREP TIME: 20 minutes › TOTAL TIME: 2 weeks

SUPPLIES

A bundle of fresh herbs

Twine, ribbon, or string

Garden snips or shears

Hooks, rope, or a vintage ladder for hanging herbs

DIRECTIONS

Cut your herbs midmorning after the dew has dried. Washing removes some of the valuable oils, so only do this if necessary. Tie their stems together with twine or string and hang them upside down in a cool, dark place. Make sure there is an inch between bundles to ensure proper airflow. Herbs with high moisture content, such as basil, mint, and tarragon, should be checked frequently for mold as they dry. Most herbs are ready for use in 2 weeks. Dried herbs are best stored in glass jars with tight-fitting lids. When using dried herbs, remember they are up to 3 times stronger than fresh herbs.

ELDERBERRY SYRUP

This syrup has been used by grandmas and homestead hippies for years to treat colds and respiratory illnesses. Our recipe even has the infamous star anise, which is the main ingredient in the cold medicine Tamiflu. Of course, health claims and remedies should be discussed with your doctor. This gets better: Not only is this simple syrup healthy, it is delicious and can be used over your pancakes, poured on ice cream, or mixed into your foodie drinks in place of bitters.

PREP TIME: 10 minutes > **TOTAL TIME: 50 minutes** > **YIELD: 16 (2 T.) servings**

DIRECTIONS

Add the water, elderberries, ginger, and star anise to a saucepan. Bring to a boil and stir in the cinnamon and cloves. Reduce to low heat and simmer for 40 minutes or until the liquid is reduced by half. Remove from the heat and strain. Cool for 10 minutes. When the liquid is lukewarm, stir in the honey. Store in an airtight jar in a cool place for up to 6 months.

INGREDIENTS

3½ cups water

⅔ cup dried elderberries

2 T. fresh grated ginger

2 whole star anise

1 tsp. cinnamon

½ tsp. ground cloves

1 cup raw honey

FIRE CIDER TONIC

Fire cider has been around for generations, and we use this folk remedy throughout the winter months or when we notice a cold coming on. Each ingredient is packed with nutritional and healing properties, so you can imagine the tonic's value when the organic apple cider vinegar is infused with all the superfoods and herbs. Peppers are hot. Words of wisdom . . . don't touch your eyes when making this, and don't let it sit too long before straining. Yes, there's a story there for another time.

PREP TIME: 30 minutes > TOTAL TIME: 3 weeks > YIELD: 16 (2 T.) servings

DIRECTIONS

Place the ginger, habaneros, garlic, and horseradish in the bottom of a large glass jar with a resealable lid. Sprinkle in the turmeric and layer the rosemary, peppercorns, cinnamon sticks, and onion. Add the lemon and orange slices, packing all the ingredients below the rim. Add the vinegar to fill the jar completely, submerging the ingredients. Seal the jar and store it in a cool place for 3 weeks. Shake the jar every other day to continue to infuse the vinegar evenly. When complete, strain it through cheesecloth into another jar and stir in the honey. If you are the gritty type, drink a shot of fire cider straight. Most prefer to dilute the tonic in water, use it with salad dressing, or even drizzle it over a bowl of chili. Store it in the refrigerator for up to 3 months.

INGREDIENTS

½ cup sliced fresh ginger, peel on

2 habanero peppers, sliced

½ cup fresh horseradish, peeled and rough chopped

1 garlic, cloves peeled

1 T. ground turmeric

3 sprigs rosemary

1 tsp. black peppercorns

2 cinnamon sticks

½ onion, cut into 6 pieces

1 lemon, sliced, peel on

1 orange, sliced, peel on

2 cups apple cider vinegar (we prefer Bragg with the "Mother")

½ cup local raw honey

SOURDOUGH STARTER

No yeast, no problem. Out of necessity, the spring of 2020 brought Zoom meetings and sourdough bread into the spotlight of society. Breads and yeast were out of stock at the grocery, and we quickly fell in love with the earthy flavors of the rustic scratch sourdough delights. Many people also find it easier to digest than yeast breads. This sourdough starter is the critical ingredient for artisan breads. You can use this bubbly starter as the base of many different breads, pancakes, muffins, and crepes. In seven short days you will be ready to bake your masterpiece.

PREP TIME: 45 minutes > TOTAL TIME: 7 days

SOURDOUGH STARTER BACKSTORY

The point of the sourdough process is the fermentation that allows your bread to rise without adding yeast. We start with whole wheat flour because that jump-starts the fermentation. Bubbles equal fermentation, and once the starter has risen and flattened out or your starter has thinned with liquid, it needs to be fed again with additional all-purpose flour and water. At first, you will feed it every 48 hours; then you will move to every 24 hours, and finally, every 12 hours.

DIRECTIONS

Days 1 and 2: Mix ½ cup whole wheat flour with ½ cup lukewarm water in a large glass jar. Use a fork to incorporate completely. It should be like thick pancake batter. Cover with plastic wrap to keep moisture in, and let it sit in a warm spot at about 75°F for 48 hours or until you see some bubbling, which is a sign of fermentation. On day 2 just wait and don't touch it.

Day 3: You should see some bubbling. Remove and discard the hooch and then remove all but ½ cup of your starter. Add ½ cup of all-purpose flour and ½ cup of lukewarm water to the starter, mix, and let this rest at room temperature for 24 hours or until the starter looks hungry. Mark the outside of the jar with a dry erase marker or a rubber band. Let it sit in a warm place on your counter.

Days 4, 5, and 6: Feed the starter 1 or 2 times a day, discarding the hooch and then all but ½ cup of starter each time. Always feed it ½ cup all-purpose flour and ½ cup lukewarm water. Look for signs that it's hungry: if it has flattened back out or if there is the hooch. Don't feed it too soon. It is better to starve it than to overfeed it.

Day 7: By now, your starter should have doubled in size and should be ready to use. You should see plenty of bubbles, both large and small. The texture will be spongy. You can name your starter, use what you need for your current recipe, and store the rest sealed in the fridge. Feed it every week to maintain it between uses.

SIDE NOTE: I'm a low-maintenance gal, so I rarely use expensive bread flour, measuring scales, or filtered water like others do. I do stir with metal utensils and use equal parts water and flour. I also use a dry-erase marker on the outside of my jar to mark the rising and falling levels. I'm such a rebel, and yet it all still works! The hooch is the liquid that develops on the top of your starter after it has risen and fallen again. It is a sign that your starter should be fed again. Pour off and discard the hooch before adding the next round of flour and water.

INGREDIENTS TO BEGIN

½ cup whole wheat flour

½ cup lukewarm water

INGREDIENTS TO FEED

5 cups all-purpose flour for daily feedings

Lukewarm water for daily feedings

FORAGED FLOWER TEA

Many beautiful wildflower blooms are edible and make wonderful teas. Whether you forage for them in the field and forest or you decide to plant an edible flower garden bed, foraged flower tea is a treat. Plenty of edible blooms are known for their medicinal qualities, but honestly, they are just plain delicious. We grow our own chamomile plants, and with this recipe, we enjoy the flowers year-round. The plant blooms all summer and into early fall, so we harvest and dry the flowers before the first frost of the season. Chamomile tea is known for its soothing properties, especially when you are feeling a sore throat coming on. A few of our other favorite tea flowers are calendula, echinacea, lavender, rose, dandelion, and hibiscus. The internet is full of information about the many surprising benefits of these natural teas. Adding the peppermint and honey is a must because of their sweet, fresh flavors and antibacterial traits.

PREP TIME: 15 minutes > TOTAL TIME: 20 minutes > YIELD: 1 Serving

INGREDIENTS

4 T. fresh edible flowers,
or 2 T. dried

1 cup boiling water

1 sprig fresh peppermint

1 tsp. honey

DIRECTIONS

To prepare the flowers, remove the heads of the flowers from the stems. Select a small sprig of mint. Begin heating water in a tea kettle. Place the flowers and your mint sprig into your tea infuser or teabag of choice. Pour 1 cup of boiling water over the flowers and mint and then steep for 5 minutes. Remove the tea infuser and discard the contents. Add honey for sweetness and start sipping.

HOMESTEAD HOT HONEY

This smoky hot honey is delicious on meat, vegetables, and breads. We use the honey straight from our Grace-Filled Homestead hives, but any local organic honey will work. This spicy sauce will make any dish better, with the added benefit of the superfood properties of raw honey.

PREP TIME: 5 minutes > TOTAL TIME: 5 minutes > YIELD: 6 Servings

DIRECTIONS

Combine all the ingredients in a bowl and mix thoroughly for 2 to 3 minutes. Store in a clean glass jar. We make our recipe very hot. If you prefer a milder version, you can cut the hot sauce in half.

INGREDIENTS

1 cup honey

2 T. smoked paprika

2 T. cayenne pepper

¼ tsp. pepper

2 T. hot sauce—we use Franks

KOMBUCHA

The effervescent kombucha drink has quickly become a trendy favorite with the hipster and health-conscious crowds. This fizzy drink is not only delicious but also good for your digestion and full of beneficial probiotics. It is economical to make yourself, and we love experimenting with different fruit flavors. Brewing your own kombucha tea is an interesting process with the starter Symbiotic Culture of Bacteria and Yeast, a.k.a. SCOBY. Everyone needs a slimy friend.

PREP TIME: 30 minutes > TOTAL TIME: 10 days > YIELD: 16 servings

DIRECTIONS

Brew black tea by heating water in a stockpot. Just before it boils, remove it from the heat and add the tea bags. Let it steep for 15 minutes. Remove the tea bags. Add the sugar and stir until it is dissolved. Let the tea cool to room temperature. Pour the tea into a gallon-sized jar with the starter tea and the SCOBY. Cover with a cotton kitchen towel or fabric secured with a rubber band. Let it sit at room temperature for 7 to 10 days where it will be undisturbed. Prepare for the second fermentation by adding about a teaspoon of dried berries to a 16 oz. swing-top glass bottle and then pour in the tea with a ladle and funnel. Repeat the process for the remaining bottles. Secure the lids and let the bottles stand at room temperature for another 3 to 7 days. You can strain out the fruit or leave it in. Refrigerate and serve.

TIPS FOR KOMBUCHA SUCCESS

• Thoroughly clean all bottles, jars, utensils, and your hands before starting, to ensure you do not introduce bad bacteria to the kombucha.

• Use high quality glass made for fermentation. This is not the time to go vintage or experiment with unusual bottles that may crack or explode.

• The fizz and pressure will build during the second fermentation. I don't recommend burping or disturbing the fermentation process, but it's important to follow the timeline and not let it go too long. As a precaution, cover the bottle with a clean dish towel when you crack it open after the second fermentation, in case the pressure builds up. This is probably not needed if you follow the timeline, but always a good idea.

• Sometimes your kombucha has floaties. This is strange at first sight, but they are your yummy and healthy friends. Either strain them out or say cheers as you down them.

• Avoid metal on the lids of your bottles because it could react to the ingredients. Glass swing-top bottles are best. Enjoy!

8 bags caffeinated black tea. (no herbal tea)

1 cup sugar

4 quarts water

1 hydrated SCOBY in 1 cup starter tea (from a friend or online)

2½ T. dried berries

QUICK VEGGIE PICKLES

Homemade quick pickles are so much easier to make than you think. This method works for all different types of veggies. They don't require your grandmother's complex canning methods. You simply make a brine, add your ingredients, and let them sit in the refrigerator. You can make your favorite vegetable into brined pickles in only 24 hours.

PREP TIME: 30 minutes > TOTAL TIME: 24 hours > YIELD: 1 (16 oz.) jar

DIRECTIONS

Start with clean jars, lids, and utensils. Prepare your desired sliced vegetables, herbs, and spices. Fill the glass jar to the top with vegetables. Then add 1 teaspoon of spices or 3 sprigs of fresh herbs. Combine all the brine ingredients and cook over medium heat until the sugar and salt dissolve. While the brine is hot, pour it directly into the jar, covering the vegetables completely. Seal the jar and let it sit out for 20 minutes before placing it in the refrigerator for 24 hours. This will slightly cook the vegetables while retaining some crunch. Store, refrigerated, for up to a month.

INGREDIENTS

1 cup water

1 cup white vinegar

2 tsp. salt

1 tsp. sugar

Flavor Combinations

Cucumber, dill, peppercorns

Beets, minced garlic, chives

Asparagus, minced garlic, dill

Mini sweet peppers, rosemary, thyme, peppercorns

Radish, ginger, turmeric, thyme, peppercorns

RECIPE INDEX

About the Author

Lana Stenner is a podcast host, college professor, backyard farmer, and the author of *The Grace-Filled Homestead*. Twenty years ago, Lana and her husband, CJ, decided to ditch their fast-paced hustle for the simple life. They found a small farm on the edge of town, moved their four little children into a 100-year-old fixer-upper, and began to focus on God, goats, and gardens at the Grace-Filled Homestead.

Follow Lana's fun barnyard animal videos on Instagram and TikTok, and draw inspiration from her recipes and DIY blog at lanastenner.com. There, you'll also discover classes at the Backyard Farm Academy and the *Grace-Filled Grit* podcast. Lana is grateful for God's grace and uses her time helping others strengthen their faith, family, and farm.

CONNECT WITH LANA

www.lanastenner.com

IG and FB @lanastenner

TikTok @lanastennerandgoatgang

Pinterest @lanastennerhomestead

Acknowledgments

I will forever be in awe of God's goodness, grace, and unending blessings that I don't deserve.

CJ (a.k.a. "the Chief")—thank you for encouraging me to continue cooking, even after I caught the apartment kitchen on fire our first week of marriage. You ripped the batteries out of the smoke detector, wiped my tears, and then washed the smoke-covered walls. We were just silly kids in love, and yet it keeps getting better. We've come a long way together, and you will always be my favorite grill master.

Kiddos—thank you for being my taste testers, cheering me on, and making me one proud mama. I love you more than life.

Mom and Dad—thank you for your love, support, and model of God's beautiful grace. You have always been my biggest cheerleaders, and I am beyond blessed to be your daughter.

Dee, close family, and friends—I truly appreciate your constant support and love. Friends that act like family are the best. It's an honor to do life with you.

Tawny—thank you for your friendship and guidance. I love your wit and insight. I will forever be grateful for you.

Jenni at Illuminate Literary—thank you for your wisdom and direction through every step of the publishing process. You are brilliant, and it's an honor to work with you.

Ruth, Hope, Heather, Adrienne, Heidi, and the Harvest House Publishers team—thank you for your friendship, insight, and vision for this book. Your encouragement, endless hours of work, and Christlike actions were visible in every single interaction. You are the real deal, and I truly appreciate you.